Barcelona

by Teresa Fisher

Barcelona is a favourite city destination for travel writer and photographer Teresa Fisher. She especially enjoys the eccentric *Modernista* architecture, the many diverse attractions and the stylish shopping. Add to this the friendliness of the Barcelonans, and it is easy to see why she is repeatedly drawn back to this vibrant and ever-changing city.

Other AA publications written by Teresa include Spiral guides to Paris, Florence and Dublin, CityPack guides to Amsterdam and Munich and, in this series, *Essential French Riviera* and *Essential Provence & the Côte d'Azur*.

Above: *blue skies over the fountain of Parc de la Ciutadella*

AA Publishing

*Barcelona has a strong
musical tradition*

Written by Teresa Fisher

First published 1999.
Reprinted 2001, verified and updated. Reprinted Sep 2001
Feb 2002
This edition 2002. Reprinted April 2003
Reprinted 2004 with amendments.
This edition 2005. Information verified and updated.
Reprinted May Oct and Nov 2005
Reprinted Jan 2006
Reprinted Apr and Aug 2006

© Automobile Association Developments Limited 2002,
2005

Published by AA Publishing, a trading name of Automobile
Association Developments Limited, whose registered
office is Fanum House, Basing View, Basingstoke,
Hampshire, RG21 4EA. Registered number 1878835.

Automobile Association Developments Limited retains the
copyright in the original edition © 1999 and in all
subsequent editions, reprints and amendments.

A CIP catalogue record for this book is available from the
British Library.

A03178

Find out more about
AA Publishing and the
wide range of travel
publications and services
the AA provides by
visiting our website at
www.theAA.com/travel

Colour separation: Pace Colour, Southampton
Printed and bound in Italy by Printer Trento Srl

Contents

About this Book 4

About this Book

KEY TO SYMBOLS

map reference to the maps in the What to See section

✉ address

☎ telephone number

🕐 opening times

🍴 restaurant or café on premises or near by

🚇 nearest underground train station

🚌 nearest bus/tram route

🚆 nearest overground train station

⛴ nearest ferry stop

♿ facilities for visitors with disabilities

✋ admission charge

↔ other places of interest near by

❓ other practical information

► indicates the page where you will find a fuller description

---

This book is divided into five sections to cover the most important aspects of your visit to Barcelona.

Viewing Barcelona pages 5–14
An introduction to Barcelona by the author.
Barcelona's Features
Essence of Barcelona
The Shaping of Barcelona
Peace and Quiet
Barcelona's Famous

Top Ten pages 15–26
The author's choice of the Top Ten places to see in Barcelona, listed in alphabetical order, each with practical information.

What to See pages 27–90
An extensive guide to Barcelona, with a brief introduction and an alphabetical listing of the main attractions, followed by a shorter guide to Catalonia.
Practical information
Snippets of 'Did you know...' information
6 suggested walks and 2 suggested drives
2 features

Where To... pages 91–116
Detailed listings of the best places to eat, stay, shop, take the children and be entertained.

Practical Matters pages 117–24
A highly visual section containing essential travel information.

Maps
All map references are to the individual maps found in the What to See section of this guide.
For example, Tibidabo has the reference ✚ 47D5 – indicating the page on which the map is located and the grid square in which the hill is to be found. A list of the maps that have been used in this travel guide can be found in the index.

Prices
Where appropriate, an indication of the cost of an establishment is given by € signs:

€€€ denotes higher prices, €€ denotes average prices, while € denotes lower charges.

Star Ratings
Most of the places described in this book have been given a separate rating:

✪✪✪   Do not miss
✪✪   Highly recommended
✪   Worth seeing

Viewing
Barcelona

Above: *Gaudí chimney faces – the 'witch-scarers' – at Casa Milà*
Right: *a proud Catalan*

5

Teresa Fisher's Barcelona

Orientating Yourself
Downtown Barcelona is
divided into distinctive
districts including *La Ribera*,
today a popular museum
quarter; *El Raval* (or *Barri
Xinès*, China Town), a rundown area with a high crime
rate (and perhaps best
avoided); the bohemian
'village' of *Grácia*;
Barceloneta, the former
fishermen's quarter; and
smart seafront developments
– *Port Vell*, the **Olympic
village** and **port**.

Below: *Christopher
Columbus surveys the
port*
Below right: *aerial view of
Passeig de Grácia – one
of Barcelona's main
thoroughfares*

Inventive and innovative, radical and racy, Barcelona is one
of Europe's most dynamic cities. Strolling through its
streets is like wandering through a living museum, a
legacy of its remarkable two thousand years of history.
From the ancient maze-like Gothic quarter, built within the
Roman city walls, to the astonishing regimental grid plan of
the turn-of-the-19th-century Eixample district, studded with
eye-catching jewels of *Modernista* architecture, and the
space-age constructions for the 1992 Olympiad, the city
contains some of the finest and most eccentric art and
architecture in the world. Outstanding even by Barcelonan
standards is Gaudí's extraordinary Sagrada Família – for
many, reason enough to visit the city.

Just as *Modernisme* – the movement that has made
Barcelona unique – emerged at the end of the 19th
century as a desire for change and renovation, so today
the city is celebrating its past. Rather than suffer a post-
Olympic slump, it is restoring its old buildings, introducing
new art and architecture and eradicating some severe
urban problems, while staying at the forefront of contemporary culture.

As a result, Barcelona today is very much alive – a city
bursting with new pride and self-confidence, which cannot
fail to excite and delight. So before you leave, consider the
city's motto – *Barcelona Es Teva* ('Barcelona Belongs to
You') – and drink from the famous Canaletes fountain on
La Rambla. It is said that after just one sip, you will fall
under the city's spell and are sure to return again, and
again...and again.

Barcelona's Features

Geography
• Barcelona is in northeastern Spain, 160km from the French border. The city occupies 99sq km, with 13km of Mediterranean coastline, including 4.2km of sandy beaches. It is bounded by the mountains of Montjuïc (to the south) and Tibidabo (to the northwest), and framed by the rivers Llobregat (to the south) and Besós (to the north).

Climate
• Barcelona enjoys a Mediterranean climate. Summers are hot and humid with an average temperature of 24°C. Winters are mild and sunny with an average temperature of 11°C. December can be very wet.

People and Economy
• Barcelona's population is 1,503,451 (or 4,264,039 within the *area metropolitana* of greater Barcelona). Many inhabitants originated from southern Spain, drawn to Catalonia in the 1950s and '60s by the prospect of work in the capital of Spain's most progressive and prosperous region.

Leisure Facilities
• Barcelona boasts 53 museums and galleries, 143 cinemas, 41 theatres, an amusement park, 2 luxury marinas, a zoo, 6 beaches, 61 parks and gardens, and over 2,300 restaurants. A special tourist bus (*Bus Turístic*) connects 18 of the most popular attractions. Thanks to the 1992 Olympics, the city has top facilities for every kind of sport.

Catalunya (Catalonia)
The autonomous region of Catalunya (Catalonia) covers an area of 31,930sq km (6.3 per cent of Spain) and has a population of over 6 million (15 per cent of the Spanish population), 70 per cent of whom live in greater Barcelona. It is Spain's leading economic region, producing 8 per cent of the country's gross national product. Nearly 40 per cent of all visitors to Spain come to Catalonia.

Above: *children play in the famous Canaletes fountain on La Rambla*

Barcelona for Wheelchair Users
Barcelona is a popular destination for wheelchair users as it is a compact city, and the modern attractions are wheelchair-friendly. However, many of the streets are cobbled, which can be uncomfortable unless appropriate tyres are fitted. The *Bus Turístic* has low-entry doors and wheelchair points, and some of the other main routes have wheelchair-accessible buses. The metro system is easy enough to get into and out of, but changing lines within it is difficult as there are generally no lifts.

Essence of Barcelona

Barcelona is unique. It has something for everyone and is one of Europe's top destinations. The only problem you will encounter is that there will never be enough time to explore its many museums and monuments, churches and galleries, its fascinating seaboard and, above all, its delectable cuisine.

Below: *the fountain in the Plaça d'Espanya*
Bottom: *aerial view of the city from the Columbus monument*

To enjoy your stay to the full, you will need to adopt the Barcelonan lifestyle – a striking blend of businesslike efficiency combined with long alfresco lunches, lazy siestas, ritual evening *passeixus* (promenades) and an intoxicating nightlife. You will long remember its proud yet generous people, who will welcome you back with open arms when you return, as you surely will.

THE **10** ESSENTIALS

If you have only a short time to visit Barcelona and would like to get a really complete picture of the city, here are the essentials:

• **Stroll along La Rambla** (➤ 23), pause for a coffee and listen to the street performers.
• **Get into Gaudí**, especially Casa Milà (➤ 37), Parc Güell (➤ 21) and the famous Sagrada Família (➤ 24–25).
• **Follow in the footsteps** of Picasso and Dalí and wander at length through the maze of narrow streets in the Barri Gòtic (➤ 38, 40).
• **Enjoy the wide variety** of *tapas* (➤ 97–100) available in the local bars.
• **Join locals to dance** the

sardana, the national dance of Catalonia (➤ 69).
• **Experience the tastes**, fragrances and colours of the Mediterranean at Mercat de la Boqueria (➤ 49).
• **Visit Museu Picasso** (➤ 20).
• **Shop for Spanish fashion** and designer gifts in the smart Eixample district (➤ 42–43).
• **Watch FC Barça play** a home match (➤ 54, 55).
• **Walk the waterfront** (➤ 70–71) and sample the freshest of seafood.

Below: *the main entrance to Parc Güell* Bottom: *human tower building in the city's Castellets festival*

The Shaping of Barcelona

c15 BC
Roman colony of Barcino founded. Roman stone city walls built in AD 4.

531
Barcelona becomes a Visigothic capital.

711
Arabs gain control of Barcelona and call it Barjelunah.

801
Barcelona seized by Franks, making it part of Charlemagne's empire.

878
Guifré el Pilós (Wilfred 'The Hairy') founds the independent county of Catalonia.

1131–62
Reign of Count Ramon Berenguer IV of Barcelona and union of Catalonia and Aragon. Barcelona becomes a major trading city.

1213–76
Reign of Jaume I.

1229
Jaume I conquers Mallorca, then Ibiza (1235), then Valencia (1238) from the Moors.

1249
Council of One Hundred (*Consell de Cent*) set up as the municipal government of Barcelona.

1298
Gothic Cathedral begun.

1323–24
Conquest of Corsica and Sardinia shows Barcelona's maritime supremacy.

1354
The *Corts Catalans*, legislative council of Catalonia, establishes the *Generalitat* to control city finances.

1355
Thousands of Jews massacred in Barcelona's *Call*.

1356
Martí I, last ruler of the House of Barcelona, dies heirless. Ineffective rule from Madrid.

1462–73
Catalan civil war. Economy deteriorates.

1492
Final expulsion of Jews. Discovery of America.

1516
Charles of Habsburg (Charles V), becomes King of Spain.

1640
Catalan *Guerra dels*

EXÉCUTION D'UN INCENDIE DE BARCELONE DANS LES FOSSÉS DE LA PRISON DE MONTJUICH

Bloody history – leaders of the Setmana Tràgica rising are executed

Segadors (Revolt of the Reapers) against Castilian rule.

1714
City falls to Franco-Spanish army during the War of the Spanish Succession. The *Nova Planta* (1715) decree abolishes Catalan institutions and Catalonia becomes a mere province of Spain.

1808–13
Departure of Napoleonic troops following five years of French occupation.

1832
Spain's first steam-driven factory opens in Barcelona.

1844
Liceu opera house opens.

1859
Cerdà's plan for the Eixample is approved.

1882
Work begins on the Sagrada Família.

1888
Universal Exhibition attracts 2 million visitors.

Late 19th to early 20th century
The Eixample district is created, containing many *Modernista* buildings.

1899
FC Barcelona founded. First electric trams.

1909
Churches and convents looted and burned by anti-establishment rioters during *Setmana Tràgica* (Tragic Week).

1914–18
Spanish neutrality in World War I helps boost Barcelona's economy.

1921
First metro line opened.

1929
International Exhibition on Montjuïc.

1931
Second Spanish Republic. Francesc Macià declares Catalan independence.

1936
Franco comes to power. His army uprising is defeated by armed city workers. Civil War starts.

1939
City falls to Nationalists. Franco's troops occupy Catalonia. Catalan language banned and Catalan culture crushed during dictatorship. Economic decline.

1975
Following Franco's death, Juan Carlos I is declared king, and acknowledges the re-establishment of the *Generalitat* as the Parliament of an autonomous regional government of Catalonia.

1992
Barcelona Olympic Games on Montjuïc.

1994
Liceu opera house gutted by fire. It reopens in 1999.

1995–96
Opening of three new museums – the Museu Nacional d'Art de Catalunya, the Museu d'Història de Catalunya and the Museu d'Art Contemporani de Barcelona – reflects continuing pride in the Catalan nation.

2002
Gaudí International Year: a variety of events, exhibitions and festivals celebrating 150 years since the birth of architect Antoni Gaudí (► 14)

2004
Barcelona hosts the Universal Forum of Cultures, sponsored by UNESCO.

The 1992 Olympics helped put Barcelona back on the world map

Peace & Quiet

Take a rest from sightseeing and visit one of the city's many beautiful parks

Barcelona is not a quiet city, yet it is always possible to find small pockets of peace – a quiet alley, a hidden square, a fountain-filled park – and the expansive greenery of Barcelona's twin mountains, Montjuïc (► 18) and Tibidabo (► 73), provides a joyful respite from frenetic city life. Alternatively, leave behind the hustle and bustle of Barcelona, and head instead for the Catalan countryside, where you will find a naturalist's paradise, blessed with more than its fair share of magnificent scenery, flora and fauna.

The Coast

Although many of the beaches in Barcelona's immediate vicinity have been spoilt, further afield lies some of the Mediterranean's most attractive coastal scenery. To the north, the charming maritime towns and villages, the warm turquoise sea, craggy cliffs and spacious sandy beaches have made the Costa Brava (wild coast) one of the most famous coastlines in Spain. Despite mass tourism, it is still possible to find small, welcoming and surprisingly unspoilt coves, their steep banks cloaked in wild flowers and cactus plants.

To the south of Barcelona, beyond the long, wide, sandy beaches of the Costa Daurada (golden coast, ► 87), running from Alcanar and Vilanova i la Geltrú, is the vast Ebro Delta – the second largest wetland habitat on the Mediterranean and home to over 300 species of bird. The area has been made a protected nature reserve, due to the importance of its wildlife and its diversity of habitats – ranging from rice paddies to sand dunes maintained by marram grass, and from riverside woods of white poplar and water-willow to freshwater lagoons framed by reeds and rushes. Look out for otters, white-toothed shrews and water voles, flamingos, purple herons, spade-foot toads, stripeless tree frogs and spiny-footed lizards.

Parc de la Ciutadella in the centre of Barcelona

The Hinterland

Catalonia's hinterland offers a variety of landscapes. Just inland from the coast, the hills are clad in Aleppo pines, stone pines and cork oaks, and splashed with the yellows and mauves of broom, gorse, heathers and orchids. Further inland, one of Catalonia's

special delights is to ramble through the region's extensive, sun-baked scrubland habitats of olives, kermes oaks and strawberry trees. The air is fragrant with lavender and wild herbs, their sweet, heady perfume attracting a busy insect life of butterflies, bugs and beetles – an endless feast for the local hoopoes, bee-eaters and warblers. Southwest of Barcelona in the Alt Penedès wine region (➤ 84–85), where the land is striped with a patchwork of tidy vines, the dramatic gorges of the Serra d'Ancosa, beyond, shelter wild boar and genets, salamanders, badgers, goshawks, tawny owls and other birds of prey.

(➤ 84–85)

Above: a complete change of scene – the impressive mountains of Ordesa National Park
Below: getting away from it all: Cardona in the foothills of the Pyrenees

The Mountains

If you have a couple of days to spare, a trip to the craggy, snow-topped Pyrenees provides a complete contrast to the Mediterranean coast surrounding Barcelona. The Aigüestortes, Estany de Sant Maurici and Ordesa National Parks provide sanctuary for chamois, wild boar and other mountain species. Glacial lagoons, jagged granite formations and verdant valleys with myriad alpine flowers and forests of sober black pine represent the quintessence of this great mountain range. One of the most important preserves of upland wildlife in Europe, the Pyrenean range is every walker's dream.

Barcelona's Famous

Arantxa Sanchez Vicario
One of Spain's greatest tennis players, Arantxa was born in Barcelona in 1971. She has won over 75 major titles, including four Grand Slam singles titles and nine Grand Slam doubles titles. Between tournaments she returns home and joins the rest of Barcelona, shopping on the Diagonal, walking her dogs in the Collserola mountains and socialising at Port Vell or Port Olímpic.

Wilfred 'The Hairy'

Few people have heard of Count Guifré 'el Pilós' (c860–98), yet not only was he the first to unite several northeastern counties, creating the basis for a future Catalan state, but he also declared Barcelona capital of the region and founded the dynasty of the Counts of Barcelona. Sadly he met an early death, in battle against the Saracens. It is said that, in recognition of his heroism, the Emperor dipped his fingers into Wilfred's bloody wounds then ran them down his golden shield, thereby creating the four red stripes of today's Catalan flag – the *Quatre Barres* (Four Bars), the oldest flag in Europe.

Antoni Gaudí

Gaudí (1852–1926), Barcelona's most famous son, occupies a unique position in the history of modern architecture. He was a true genius of the *Modernista* movement, without predecessor or successor. To this day his flamboyant art is unique. For many people, Gaudí alone is sufficient reason to visit Barcelona, to see his remarkable organic structures, his trademark pinnacles, towers and rooftop terraces and, above all, the church of the Sagrada Família (➤ 24–25). Tragically, Gaudí was run over by a tram on the Gran Via and died unrecognised in hospital. When his identity was discovered, Barcelona gave him what was almost a state funeral.

Pablo Ruiz Picasso

Málaga-born Picasso (1881–1973) spent many of his formative years (from the age of 14 to 23) in Barcelona, and is said to have considered himself more Catalan than Andalucian. He was particularly fond of the Catalan capital and, even after his move to Paris in 1904, continued to visit Barcelona regularly, until the Civil War (the subject of his famous painting, *Guernica*) put an end to his visits. Museu Picasso (➤ 20), the city's most visited museum, is particularly rich in paintings from his Barcelona period.

Left: *Picasso never forgot his early adulthood spent in Barcelona*
Above left: *Arantxa Sanchez Vicario*

Top Ten

Above: *Casa Bruno Quadras on La Rambla*
Right: *Gaudí ironwork*

15

1
Catedral

✝ 62C3

✉ Plaça de la Seu 3

☎ 93 310 71 95

🕐 Daily 8–1:15, 5–7:30

Ⓜ Jaume I

🚌 17, 19, 40, 45

♿ Few

🆓 Free

↔ Ciutat Vella (➤ 38–39);
Museu Frederic Marès
(➤ 55)

Museum

☎ 93 315 22 13

🕐 Daily 10–12:45, 5–6:45

🆓 Cheap

❓ Small gift shop

Barcelona's great cathedral is not only one of the most celebrated examples of Catalan Gothic style, but also one of the finest cathedrals in Spain.

The cathedral is located at the heart of the Barri Gòtic (➤ 40), on the remains of an early Christian basilica and a Romanesque church. Most of the building was erected between the late 13th century and the middle of the 15th century, although the heavily ornate main façade and octagonal dome were constructed at the beginning of the 20th century.

The impressive interior represents a harmonious blend of Medieval and Renaissance styles, with a lofty triple nave, graceful arches, 29 side chapels and an intricately carved choir. Beneath the main altar is the crypt of Santa Eulàlia (the patron saint of Barcelona), which contains her tomb.

Near the main entrance is the Chapel of Christ of Lepanto (formerly the Chapter House), which is widely considered to be the finest example of Gothic art in the cathedral. It contains the crucifix carried on board *La Real*, the flagship of Don Juan of Austria (➤ 41), during the famous Battle of Lepanto. The 14th-century cloister is the

most beautiful part of the cathedral, its garden of magnolias, palms and fountains making a cool retreat from the heat of Barcelona. There is even a small pond, with a flock of white geese, supposedly symbolising Santa Eulàlia's virginal purity. A small **museum** just off the cloister shelters many of the cathedral's most precious treasures.

Despite its grandeur, the cathedral remains very much a people's church. Worshippers outnumber tourists and on Sundays Barcelonans gather in Plaça de la Seu at noon to perform the *sardana*, a stately Catalan folk dance which symbolises unity (➤ 69).

Soaring arches in the great cathedral

2
Fundació Joan Miró

This dazzling gallery pays homage to Joan Miró, one of Catalonia's greatest artists, famous for his childlike style and use of vibrant colours.

Vibrant colours typify Miró's work

Fragment of the Tapis de la Fundació Joan Miró, Joan Miró © ADAGP, Paris and DACS, London 1998

The Miró Foundation was set up by Joan Miró in 1971, and is devoted to the study of his works and to the promotion of all contemporary art. The gallery – a modern building of white spaces, massive windows and skylights designed by Josep Lluís Sert – is itself a masterpiece and a perfect place in which to pursue the Foundation's aims. It contains some 200 Mirónian paintings, 153 sculptures, nine tapestries, his complete graphic works and over 5,000 drawings, making it one of the world's most complete collections of this great master.

Miró was born in Barcelona in 1893 and, apart from a brief spell in Paris, spent most of his life in the city developing his bold style of vigorous lines and intense primary colours. In 1956 he moved to Mallorca, and remained on the island until his death in 1983.

Highlights of the gallery include some of Miró's earliest sketches, the tapestry *Tapis de la Fundació* and a set of black-and-white lithographs entitled *Barcelona Series* (1939–44) – an artistic appraisal of the war years. The roof terrace and gardens contain several striking sculptures.

The Foundation also presents temporary exhibitions of modern art, contemporary music recitals (▶ 114) and a special permanent collection called 'To Joan Miró', with works by Ernst, Tàpies, Calder and Matisse among others, a touching tribute to the person and his work.

✚ 28C2

✉ Avinguda de Miramar, Parc de Montjuïc

☎ 93 443 94 70

🕐 Oct–Jun Tue–Sat 10–7, Thu till 9:30; Jul–Sep Tue–Sat 10–8, Thu till 9:30; Sun & hols 10–2:30

🍴 Café-restaurant (€€)

Espanya 🚌 50, 55

♿ Good ✋ Expensive

17

3
Montjuïc

🔲 28C1

🍴 Cafés and restaurants
(€–€€)

Ⓜ Espanya

🚌 50, 51

🚋 Montjuïc funicular from
Paral.lel Metro

✋ Free

↔ Anella Olímpica (► 32)

Few can resist the charms of the city's local hill, with its museums, galleries, gardens and other attractions set in an oasis of natural calm.

The history of Montjuïc, a 213m-high hill south of the city and the dominant feature of its coast and skyline, has been linked to the city's history since prehistoric times. The Romans later called it 'Jove's Mountain' but today it is called 'Mountain of the Jews', after an early Jewish necropolis here. The castle, standing on the bluff, dates from the 16th to 18th centuries and houses the **Museu Militar**, exhibiting collections of military weaponry and uniforms from different countries and periods.

Museums

📞 Museu Militar: 93 329
86 13; Museu
Arqueològic: 93 424 65
77; Museu Etnològic: 93
424 64 02;

🕐 Tue–Sun, times vary

✋ Cheap; Museo Etnològic
free first Sun of month

Above: *view of Montjuïc
from the Columbus
monument*

18

In 1929 Montjuic was the venue for the International Expo. Today many of its buildings are filled with museums. The **Museu Arqueològic** and the **Museu Etnològic** typify the Expo's architecture, as does the Palau Nacional, home of the Museu Nacional d'Art de Catalunya (► 19).

Beneath the Palau Nacional, Plaça d'Espanya marks the main entrance to the Expo with Venetian towers, and an avenue leading to Plaça de la Font Màgica – 'Magic Fountain' – a spectacular sight that always draws the crowds. The road continues up past the Pavello Barcelona (► 66) and the Poble Espanyol (► 22) to Fundació Joan Miró (► 17) and the Anella Olímpica (► 32), venue for much of the 1992 Olympic Games.

4

Museu Nacional d'Art de Catalunya (MNAC)

Dominating the northern flank of Montjuïc, this imposing neoclassical palace contains a treasure trove of Catalan art spanning several centuries.

The National Museum of Catalan Art is one of the best museums of medieval art in the world. Housed in an extravagant National Exhibition building, built as the symbol of the 1929 World Exhibition (► 22), the museum is currently undergoing renovation by architect Gae Aulenti, who also converted the Gare d'Orsay into one of Paris's foremost museums.

The MNAC boasts the world's most eminent Romanesque art collection, with stone sculptures, wood carvings, gold and silverwork, altar cloths, enamels and coins and a beautifully presented series of 11th- and 12th-century murals, carefully stripped from church walls throughout Catalonia and precisely reconstructed in apses, as if they were still in their original locations.

The idea for this collection originated in the early 20th century when the theft of national architectural treasures in Catalonia was at its height, necessitating a church-led crusade to move some of the region's most precious treasures to a safe location.

The museum's Gothic collection forms a striking contrast with over 400 highly ornate retables and sculptures, including an extraordinary 15th-century Virgin in full flamenco dress. A somewhat fragmented collection of Renaissance and baroque paintings embraces works by Tintoretto, El Greco and Zurbarán.

The museum also contains the Museum of Drawings and Prints, the Numismatic Museum of Catalonia, the Museu d'Art Modern (► 54), which moved here from the Ciutadella Park in 2004, and will eventually house the General Library of Art History.

✚	28C2
✉	Palau Nacional, Parc de Montjuïc
☎	93 622 03 76
🕐	Tue–Sat 10–7; Sun and hols 10–2:30. Closed Mon
🍴	Café-bar (€)
🚇	Espanya
🚌	9, 13, 30, 50, 55
♿	Excellent
✋	Expensive; free first Thu of month
↔	Anella Olímpica (► 32)

The MNAC – a treasure house of Barcelonan history

19

5
Museu Picasso

Below and bottom: the Museu Picasso draws thousands of vistors

This fascinating museum traces the career of the most acclaimed artist of modern times, from early childhood sketches to the major works of later years.

The Picasso Museum is the city's biggest tourist attraction. It contains one of the world's most important collections of Picasso's work and until 2003, when the impressive Museo Picasso Málaga opened in his birthplace, was the only one of significance in his native country.

Pablo Ruiz Picasso was born in Andalucia, but moved to the Catalan capital in 1895, aged 14. He was an exceptionally gifted artist and, by the time of his first exhibition in 1900, was well known. In 1904 he moved to Paris, but remained in contact with Barcelona.

The museum contains work from his early years, notably a series of impressionistic landscapes and seascapes, a portrait of his aunt, Tía Pepa (1896), notebook sketches and paintings of street scenes, including *Sortida del Teatre* (1896) and *La Barceloneta* (1897), and the menu for *Els Quatre Gats* (Four Cats) café (► 94). Other works are from the Blue Period (1901–1904), the Pink Period (1904–1906), the Cubist (1907–20) and Neo-classical (1920–25) periods, through to the mature works of later years. There are also 41 ceramic pieces donated by his wife, Jacqueline in 1982, which graphically demonstrate Picasso's astonishing artistic development.

✚ 29E4

✉ Carrer Montcada 15–23

☎ 93 319 63 10

🕐 Tue–Sat and hols 10–8, Sun 10–3. Closed Mon

🍴 Café-restaurant (€€)

Ⓜ Jaume I

🚌 14, 17, 19, 36, 39, 40 45, 51, 57, 59, 64, 157

♿ Very good

✋ Expensive (free first Sun of month)

↔ Museu Tèxtil i d'Indumentària (► 57)

6
Parc Güell

Deemed a failure in its day, Gaudí's eccentric hilltop park is now considered one of the city's treasures and a unique piece of landscape design.

The architectural work of Gaudí is inseparable from Barcelona, largely thanks to his relationship with the Güells, a family of industrialists who commissioned from him a number of works. For Parc Güell, Don Eusebi Güell, Gaudí's main patron, had grand ideas for a residential English-style garden city, with 60 houses set in formal gardens. Gaudí worked on the project from 1900 to 1914, but it proved an economic disaster: only three houses were completed, and the park became city property in 1923.

The park's main entrance is marked by two eccentric pavilions. A grand stairway, ornamented by a dragon fountain, leads to a massive cavernous space, originally intended as the marketplace. Its forest of pillars supports a rooftop plaza bordered by a row of curved benches, covered in multicoloured *trencadís* (broken ceramics).

Throughout the 20 hectares of Mediterranean-style parkland, there are sculptures, steps and paths raised on columns of 'dripping' stonework. Gaudí himself lived in one of the houses from 1906 to 1926. Built by his pupil Berenguer, it is now the Casa-Museu Gaudí (☎ 93 219 38 11) and contains models, furniture, drawings and other memorabilia of the architect and his colleagues.

✠ 47D4

✉ Main entrance: Carrer Olot

☎ 93 213 04 88

🕐 Daily May–Aug 10–9, Sep & Apr 10–8, Oct & Mar 10–7, Nov–Feb 10–6

🍴 Self-service bar

🚇 Lesseps or Vallcarca (and uphill walk)

🚌 24, 25, 28, 87

✋ Free

↔ Hospital de la Santa Creu i Sant Pau (➤ 45); Parc de la Creueta del Coll (➤ 65)

Sit on one of Europe's most unusual park benches

7
Poble Espanyol

This charming Andalucian square is the centrepiece of the Poble Espanyol

You can tour the whole of Spain in an afternoon here at Barcelona's 'Spanish Village', a remarkable showcase of regional architectural styles.

✠ 28B2

✉ Avinguda de Marqués de Comillas s/n

☎ 93 508 63 30

🕐 Mon 9AM–8PM; Tue–Thu 9AM–2AM; Fri & Sat 9AM–4AM; Sun 9AM–noon

🍴 Plenty (€–€€)

Ⓜ Espanya

🚌 13, 50

♿ Only partially accessible to wheelchair users, who have free entry

✋ Expensive

↔ Anella Olímpica (➤ 32); Fundació Joan Miró (➤ 17); Montjuïc (➤ 18); Museu Nacional d'Art de Catalunya (➤ 19)

Built for the 1929 World Exhibition, the Poble Espanyol (Spanish Village) was intended as a re-creation of the diversity of Spanish regional architecture through the ages. It could easily have resembled a stage set or a theme park, but instead, the 115 life-sized reproductions of buildings, clustered around 6 squares and 3km of streets, form an authentic village, where visitors can identify famous or characteristic buildings ranging from the patios of Andalucia to Mallorcan mansions and the granite façades of Galicia.

Within the village are bars and restaurants serving regional specialities, and over 60 shops selling folk crafts and regional artefacts. Some are undeniably over-priced, but there are also some real finds (➤ 107).

The Museum of Popular Arts, Industries and Traditions and the Museum of Graphic Arts are also located here and every Sunday at midday, a *festa* enlivens the main square.

The Poble Espanyol was smartened up for the 1992 Olympics, with the introduction of 'The Barcelona Experience' (a half-hour audio-visual history of the city) and several restaurants and bars, including the extraordinary Torres de Ávila (➤ 113), a trendy 'designer bar'-cum-nightclub, one of Barcelona's hottest night spots. Excellent flamenco shows can also be seen at El Tablao de Carmen (➤ 114).

8
La Rambla

Sooner or later, every visitor joins the locals swarming day and night down La Rambla, the most famous walkway in Spain.

Life on Barcelona's most famous street is never dull

The name La Rambla, derived from *ramla* (Arabic for 'torrent'), serves as a reminder that in earlier times, the street was a sandy gully that ran parallel to the medieval wall, and carried rainwater down to the sea. Today's magnificent 18th-century tree-lined walkway, running through the heart of the old city down to the port, is the pride of Barcelona. The central promenade is split into various distinctive sections strung head-to-tail, each with their own history and characteristics, from the flower stalls along Rambla de les Flors to the birdcages of Rambla dels Ocells (Walk, ➤ 51). And it is said if you drink from the famous fountain (➤ 51) in La Rambla de Canaletes you are sure to return to the city.

Promenading La Rambla is never the same twice, changing with the seasons, by the day and by the hour. It's an experience eagerly shared by people from every walk of life – tourists, locals, bankers, Barça fans, artists, beggars, street-performers, newspaper-sellers, pickpockets, night-clubbers, students, lovers and theatre crowds – all blending together with the noise of the traffic, the birdsong, the buskers, and the scent of the flowers. Such is the significance to the city of this promenade *par excellence*, that two words – *ramblejar* (a verb meaning 'to walk down the Rambla') and *ramblista* (an adjective describing someone addicted to the act of *ramblejar*) – have been adopted in its honour.

➕ 29D3

🍴 Plenty (€–€€€)

Ⓜ Catalunya, Drassanes, Liceu

🚌 14, 38, 59, 91

🚢 Boat excursions from Moll de les Drassanes (➤ 110)

↔ Ciutat Vella (➤ 38–39); Drassanes and Museu Marítim (➤ 41); Mercat de la Boqueria (➤ 49); Palau Güell (➤ 57); Plaça de Catalunya (➤ 67); Plaça Reial (➤ 69)

❓ Sant Jordi (St George's Day) celebrations on 23 April (➤ 116. panel). Beware of pickpockets

9
La Sagrada Família

Opposite and below: the Sagrada Família must be seen to be believed

Big Ben, the Eiffel Tower...most cities have a distinctive monument. Barcelona has Gaudí's Sagrada Família, his, as yet unfinished, cathedral.

✚ 29E6

✉ Plaça Sagrada Família

☎ 93 207 30 31

🕐 Daily Apr–Sep 9–8, Oct–Mar 9–6

🚇 Sagrada Familia

🚌 19, 33, 34, 43, 44, 50, 51, 54

♿ Few

✋ Expensive (additional charge for lift)

↔ L'Eixample (► 42–43); Hospital de la Santa Creu i Sant Pau (► 45)

❓ Crypt museum, gift shop, lift and stairway to the towers

Antoni Gaudí, the internationally prestigious figure of Catalan architecture, started work on La Sagrada Família (Temple of the Holy Family) in 1882, and for the latter part of his life dedicated himself entirely to his great vision for Europe's biggest cathedral. His dream was to include three façades representing the birth, death and resurrection of Christ, and eighteen mosaic-clad towers symbolising the Twelve Apostles, the four Evangelists, the Virgin Mary, and Christ. On his untimely death in 1926 (► 14), only the crypt, one of the towers, the majority of the east (Nativity) façade, and the apse were completed. Ever since, the fate of the building has been the subject of often bitter debate.

With a further estimated 80 years of work (which would include the destruction of several buildings in Carrer Mallorca and Carrer Valencia), it seems that the Sagrada Família will probably never be more than a shell. Even as it stands today, it has become a world-wide symbol of Barcelona, one of the great architectural wonders of the world, and a must on every visitor's itinerary.

10
Santa Maria del Mar

✝ 29E4

✉ Plaça de Santa Maria

☎ 93 310 23 90

🕐 Daily 9–1:30, 4:30–8
(from 10AM Sun)

🚇 Barceloneta, Jaume I

🚌 14, 17, 36, 39, 40, 45,
51, 57, 59, 64, 157

♿ Good   ✋ Free

↔ Museu Picasso (➤ 20);
Palau de Mar (➤ 58)

Right and below: *Santa
Maria epitomises Catalan
Gothic architecture*

*Barcelona's seaside cathedral is a Gothic triumph,
built to demonstrate Catalan supremacy in
Mediterranean commerce.*

The 14th-century church of Santa Maria del Mar (St Mary
of the Sea) is located at the heart of La Ribera (The
Waterfront), the medieval city's maritime and trading
district. This neighbourhood's link with the sea dates back
to the 10th century, when a settlement grew up along the
seashore outside the city walls, around a chapel called
Santa Maria de les Arenes (St Mary of the Sands). During
the 13th century, the settlement grew and became known
as Vilanova de Mar. Its identity was eventually firmly
established with the transformation of the tiny chapel into
the magnificent church of Santa Maria del Mar, built on
what was then the seashore, as a show of maritime
wealth and power. Indeed, the foundation stone
commemorated the Catalan conquest of Sardinia.

The church was built between 1329 and 1384 and has a
purity of style that makes it one of the finest examples of
Barcelona's Gothic heritage. The plain exterior is charac-
terised by predominantly horizontal lines and two
octagonal, flat-roofed towers. Inside, the wide, soaring
nave and high, narrow aisles, all supported by slim,
octagonal columns, provide a great sense of spaciousness.
Sadly, the ornaments of the side chapels were lost when
the city was besieged, once by Bourbon troops in 1714
and again during the Spanish Civil War. The resulting
bareness of the interior, apart from the sculpture of a 15th-
century ship that sits atop the altar, enables you to admire
the church's striking simplicity without distraction.

What to See

Above: *chimney detail on Gaudi's Casa Mila*
Right: *street entertainer on La Rambla*

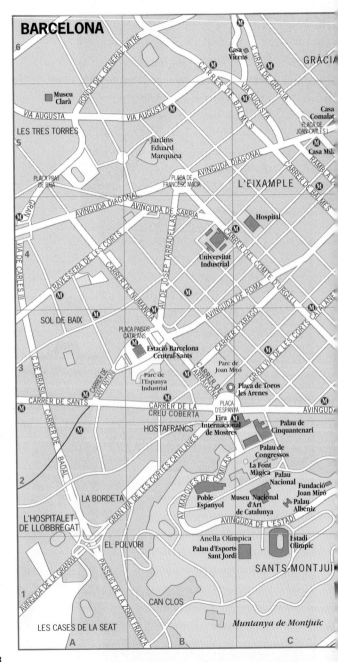

BARCELONA

GRÀCIA

Casa Vicens

Casa Comalat

PLAÇA DE JOAN CARLES I

Casa Milà

Museu Clarà

VIA AUGUSTA

VIA AUGUSTA

LES TRES TORRES

Jardins Eduard Marquina

RONDA DEL GENERAL MITRE

CARRER DE GRACIA

CARRER DE BALMES

VIA AUGUSTA

RAMBLA D

CARRER DE BALMES

PLAÇA PRAT DE RIBA

PLAÇA DE FRANCESC MACIÀ

AVINGUDA DIAGONAL

L'EIXAMPLE

GRAN VIA

VIA DE CARLES III

AVINGUDA DIAGONAL

AVINGUDA DE SARRIA

Hospital

CARRER DEL COMTE D'URGELL

TRAVESSERA DE LES CORTS

CARRER DE LES CORTS

CARRER DE NUMANCIA

AV DE JOSEP TARRADELLAS

Universitat Industrial

CATALAN

AVINGUDA DE ROMA

SOL DE BAIX

CARRER D'ARAGÓ

GRAN VIA DE LES CORTS

PLAÇA PAISOS CATALANS

Estació Barcelona Central-Sants

C. DE BRASIL

CARRER DE SANTS

CARRER DE

BADAL

CARRER DE SANTALLO

Parc de l'Espanya Industrial

CARRER DE TARRAGONA

Parc de Joan Miró

Plaça de Toros les Arenes

AVINGUDA

CARRER DE LA CREU COBERTA

PLAÇA D'ESPANYA

Fira Internacional de Mostres

HOSTAFRANCS

Palau de Cinquantenari

GRAN VIA DE LES CORTS CATALANES

AV MARQUES DE COMILLAS

Palau de Congressos

La Font Màgica

Palau Nacional

Fundació Joan Miró

LA BORDETA

Poble Espanyol

Museu Nacional d'Art de Catalunya

Palau Albéniz

L'HOSPITALET-DE LLOBBREGAT

AVINGUDA DE L'ESTADI

EL POLVORÍ

Anella Olímpica

Palau d'Esports Sant Jordi

Estadi Olímpic

SANTS-MONTJUI

AVINGUDA DE LA GRANJA

PASSEIG DE LA ZONA FRANCA

CAN CLOS

LES CASES DE LA SEAT

Muntanya de Montjuïc

A   B   C

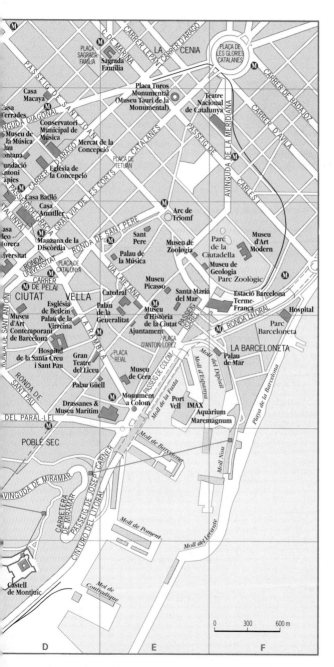

Barcelona

Ever since it was founded over 2,000 years ago, Barcelona has been striving to become a great metropolis. To its inhabitants, it is not Spain's second city but the capital of Catalonia; not a Spanish metropolis but a European one, and the Spanish leader in both *haute couture* and *haute cuisine*. The best time to see Barcelona in its true colours is after FC Barça wins an important match, and the streets erupt with excitement to the sound of car horns and popping champagne corks.

Visitors to Barcelona, on the other hand, are entranced by the Mediterranean atmosphere of the city, the richness of its art and architectural treasures both ancient and modern, the proud but not narrowly nationalistic character of the people, the strong tradition of theatre and music and the exuberant nightlife. In this dynamic and passionate city, it is easy to live life to the full, both day and night.

> *'I would rather be Count of Barcelona than King of the Romans.'*
>
> CHARLES V
> *Holy Roman Emperor (1519)*

The City of Barcelona

Barcelona is easy to get to know. It is a compact city, small enough to explore on foot but great enough to be enormously varied. Most of the main sights are in three main areas: the Ciutat Vella (Old City), the Eixample and the Waterfront.

It is easy to lose yourself in the hidden corners of the Old City, to stumble upon a colourful market in a fountain-splashed square, to explore the city's boutiques, or to write some postcards in the geese-filled cloisters of the cathedral. The Eixample is particularly remarkable for the way the great turn-of-the-19th-century Modernists (*Modernistas*) created some of the most imaginative and bizarre buildings in the world within the confines of a rigid grid system of streets.

The city has often been accused of ignoring the sea on which so much of its fame and prosperity depended. The extension of the seafront began with the naming of Barcelona as host city for the 1992 Olympics. Today, with its smart coastal promenades, sandy beaches, and a plethora of open-air bars and restaurants, Barcelona's image is 'Cara al Mar' ('Face to the Sea'). Leading from the seafront, La Rambla is a must-see, a bustling avenue of cafés, bookstalls and flower kiosks, the best place to people-watch and to feel the city's true pulse. By contrast, twin hills Montjuïc and Tibidabo provide a welcome refuge from downtown Barcelona, with their panoramic views over the rooftops to the Pyrenean mountains beyond and the sparkling Mediterranean sea.

Below: *buskers on La Rambla*
Bottom: *Avinguda Portal de l'Angel, a popular shopping precinct*

What to See in Barcelona

L'ANELLA OLÍMPICA ✪✪

In 1992, Montjuïc mountain (► 18) was temporarily renamed 'Mount Olympus' and became Barcelona's main venue for the Olympic Games. Atop its western crest lies the Anella Olímpica (Olympic Ring), a monumental complex of concrete and marble that contains some of the city's most celebrated new buildings: Ricardo Bofills' neo-classical sports university; the Institut Nacional de Educació Física de Catalunya (INEFC); the Complex Esportiu Bernat Picornell swimming-pool complex; Santiago Calatrava's space-age communications tower, which dominates the skyline; and the remarkable black steel and glass domed Palau de Sant Jordi, designed by Japanese architect Arata Isozaki, which looks more like a UFO than a covered sports stadium.

Barcelona had bid for the games three times previously and had built Europe's biggest stadium for the 1929 World Exhibition with the clear intention of using it for the 1936 'People's Olympics' (organised as an alternative to the Nazi's infamous Berlin Games). These never took place due to the outbreak of Spanish Civil War the day before the official opening. For the 1992 games, local architects managed to preserve the stadium's original façade, while increasing the seating capacity from 25,000 to 70,000 by excavating deep into the interior. Today, highlights of the 1992 games can be relived through video clippings and souvenir showcases in the **Galería Olímpica**, located beneath the stadium.

✚ 34C3

✉ Avinguda de l'Estadi/Passeig Olímpic, Montjuïc

☎ Estadi Olímpic: 93 426 20 89; Palau Sant Jordi: 93 426 20 89; Picornell swimming pools: 93 423 4041

🚇 Espanya, or Paral.lel, then Funicular de Montjuïc

🚌 61

♿ Very good

🎟 Free

Galería Olímpica

☎ 93 426 06 60

🕐 Apr–Sep Mon–Fri 10–2, 4–7; rest of year by appointment for groups of more than 15

🚌 61

♿ Good

🎟 Cheap

Above: the stadium that hosted the XXVth Olympic and the IXth Paralympic Games

LA BARCELONETA AND PORT OLÍMPIC ✪✪

Following the siege and conquest of Barcelona by Felipe V in 1714, a large area of the Ribera district was destroyed to make way for a new citadel (➤ 64, Did You Know?). The displaced residents lived for years in makeshift shelters on the beach, until in 1755 a new district was developed on a triangular wedge of reclaimed land between the harbour and the sea, named La Barceloneta (Little Barcelona).

In the 19th century, La Barceloneta became home to seamen and dockers and it is still very much a working district, retaining its distinctive shanty-town atmosphere, fishy smells, and a quayside lined with the boats and nets of the local fleet. Today most visitors come here to eat in the many fine seafood eateries (*chiringuitos*), in particular those along the main harbourside thoroughfare, Passeig Joan de Borbó, and the restaurants of the converted Palau de Mar warehouse (➤ 58).

By contrast, Port Olímpic, with its smart promenades and glittering new marina, has given new impetus to Barcelona's nautical activities. Its chic restaurants, cafés and bars have become a lively night spot for both locals and tourists. Spain's two tallest buildings preside over the port – the office-filled Torre Mapfre and the five-star hotel Arts Barcelona, Barcelona's top hotel (➤ 101). Near by, a striking bronze fish sculpture (➤ 71, 74) by Frank Gehry (architect of the Guggenheim Museum in Bilbao) heralds the start of the Passeig Marítim, which links the port with La Barceloneta and extends 8km to Sant Adrià del Besòs.

Hotel Arts and Gehry's Fish – symbols of a new and progressive city

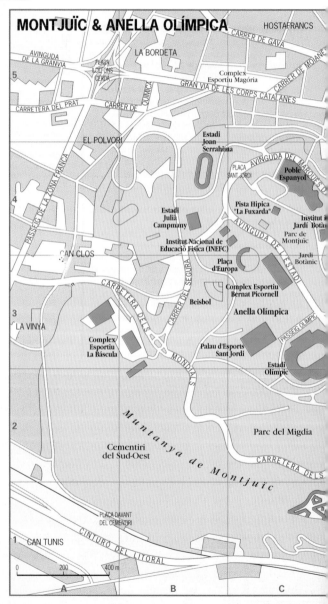

MONTJUÏC & ANELLA OLÍMPICA

HOSTAFRANCS

CARRER DE GAVA

AVINGUDA DE LA GRANVIA

LA BORDETA

PLAÇA ILDEFONS CERDA

Complex Esportiu Magória

CARRER DE MOIANE

GRAN VIA DE LES CORPS CATALANES

5

QUIMICA

CARRETERA DEL PRAT

CARRER DE

EL POLVORI

Estadi Joan Serrahima

AVINGUDA DEL MARQUES D

PLAÇA SANT JORDI

Poble Espanyol

4

PASSEIG DE LA ZONA FRANCA

Estadi Julià Campmany

Pista Hipica "La Fuxarda"

Institut Jardí Botà

AVINGUDA DE L'ESTADI

Parc de Montjuic

Institut Nacional de Educació Física (INEFC)

CAN CLOS

Plaça d'Europa

Jardi Botànic

CARRER DE SEGURA

Complex Esportiu Bernat Picornell

LA VINYA

CARRETERA DELS

Beisbol

Anella Olímpica

3

PASSEIG OLÍMPIC

Complex Esportiu La Bàscula

MONDIALS

Palau d'Esports Sant Jordi

Estadi Olímpic

2

M u n t a n y a

d e

M o n t j u ï c

Parc del Midgia

Cementiri del Sud-Oest

CARRETERA DELS

PLAÇA DAVANT DEL CEMENTIRI

1

CAN TUNIS

CINTURO DEL LITORAL

0   200   400 m

A   B   C

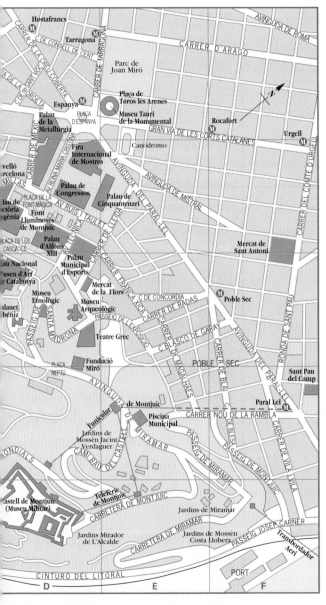

Hostafrancs

Tarragona

CARRER D'ARAGO

AVINGUDA DE ROMA

C DE CONSELL DE CENT

CARRER DE LA PRIEI COBERTA

CARRER DE TARRAGONA

Parc de
Joan Miró

DE LA BORDETA

SANT ROCE

Plaça de
Toros les Arenes

Espanya

CARRER DE MEXIC

Palau
de la
Metallúrgia

PLAÇA
D'ESPANYA

Museu Tauri
de la Monumental

Rocafort

Urgell

AV REINA MARIA CRISTINA

GRAN VIA DE LES CORTS CATALANES

CARRER DEL COMTE D'URGELL

velló
rcelona

MILLAS

Fira
Internacional
de Mostres

Canodromo

Palau de
Congressos

PLAÇA DE LA
FONT MÀGICA

ïau de
ctòria
gènia

Font
Lluminoses
de Montjuïc

AV RUIS I TAULET

Palau de
Cinquantenari

AVINGUDA DEL PARAL-LEL

AVINGUDA DE MISTRAL

AÇA DE LES
CASCADES

Palau
d'Alfons
XIII

Palau
Municipal
d'Esports

Mercat de
Sant Antoni

CARRER DE LLEIDA

au Nacional

useu d'Art
e Catalunya

Mercat
de la Flors

C DE CONCORDIA

Poble Sec

alauet
béniz

Museu
Etnològic

Museu
Arqueològic

PASSEIG DE L'EXPOSICIO

CARRER DE RADAS

CARRER DE LA

RONDA DE SANT PAU

SANTA MADRONA

Teatre Grec

C. BLASCO DE GARAY

POBLE SEC

PASSEIG

Fundació
Miró

CARRER DE MIGALHAES

CARRER DE BLAI

AVINGUDA DEL PARAL-LEL

Sant Pau
del Camp

PLAÇA
NEPTÚ

AVINGUDA

DE MONTJUIC

Piscina
Municipal

CARRER NOU DE LA RAMBLA

Paral-Lel

Funicular

Jardins de
Mossèn Jacint
Verdaguer

PASSEIG DE MIRAMAR

PASSEIG DE BLESSEIG DE MONTJUÏC

CARRER DE VILA VILA

ONDIALS

CAMÍ BAIX DEL CASTELL

Telefèric
de Montjuïc

CARRETERA DE MONTJUIC

Jardins de Miramar

astell de Montjuïc
(Museu Militar)

Jardins Mirador
de L'Alcalde

CARRETERA DE MIRAMAR

Jardins de Mossèn
Costa Llobera

PASSEIG JOSEP CARNER

Transbordador
Aeri

CINTURÓ DEL LITORAL

PORT

D

E

F

35

29D4
Passeig de Gràcia 41
93 488 01 39
Mon–Sat 10–7, Sun 10–2
Passeig de Gràcia
Good
Free
Eixample (➤ 42–43);
Fundació Antoni Tàpies
(➤ 44)
The entrance hall, open
to the public, contains the
information centre for *La
Ruta del Modernisme*

29D4
Passeig de Gràcia 43
93 488 06 66/93 488 30
90
Daily 9–8; ticket office
9–1:30
Passeig de Gràcia
Good
Expensive
Eixample (➤ 42–43);
Fundació Antoni Tàpies
(➤ 44)

CASA AMATLLER ✪

Chocolate manufacturer Antonio Amatller i Costa commissioned Josep Puig i Cadafalch to remodel Casa Amatller
into an extravagant home with a neo-Gothic façade
decorated with sculptures, coats of arms and floral reliefs,
and crowned by a stepped gable. Inside the broad
entranceway, the beautiful wooden lift was one of
Barcelona's earliest elevators. Note also the amazing
carvings on one interior doorway depicting animals making
chocolate. A combined ticket is available for a guided tour,
La Ruta del Modernisme, which includes the three façades
of Casa Amatller, Casa Batlló and Casa Lleó-Morera and
discounted entry to attractions.

CASA BATLLÓ ✪✪✪

Casa Batlló is one of the most famous buildings of the
Modernista school, designed by Gaudí for Josep Batlló i
Casanovas and completed in 1907. It is said to illustrate
the triumph of Sant Jordi (St George) over the dragon, with
its mosaic façade, covered in glazed blue, green and ochre
ceramics, representing the scaly skin of the dragon, its
knobbly roof the dragon's back, the tower the saint's
cross, and the wave-like balconies the skulls and bones
of victims.

*Casa Batlló – Gaudí's
famous 'dragon' building*

CASA LLEÓ-MORERA ✪✪

This striking *Modernista* building is considered Lluís Domènech i Montaner's most exuberant decorative work. Its flamboyant façade cleverly minimises the corner by placing visual emphasis on ornate circular balconies, columned galleries and oriel windows. Inside, a florid pink mosaic vestibule and open staircase lead to first-floor living quarters, lavishly decorated with stencilled stuccowork, stained glass, marquetry and mosaics, portraying roses (the nationalist symbol of Catalonia), lions (*lleó*) and mulberry bushes (*morera*). It is closed to the public.

CASA MILÀ ✪✪

Known locally as La Pedrera (the quarry), Spain's most controversial apartment block and Antoni Gaudí's last and most famous secular building was built between 1906 and 1912 and shows this great Catalan architect at his most inventive. It also shows Gaudí's genius as a structural engineer, with seven storeys built entirely on columns and arches, supposedly without a single straight line or right-angled corner. Its most distinctive features are the rippling limestone façade, with its intricate ironwork, and the strangely shaped chimneys of the roof terrace.

After years of neglect, Casa Milà was declared a World Heritage Site by UNESCO in 1984, and purchased by the Caixa Catalunya Foundation, which invested over 8,000 million pesetas to restore it to its original glory.

CATEDRAL (► 16, TOP TEN)

🟥 29D4
✉ Passeig de Gràcia 35
☎ No phone
🕐 Interior currently not open to the public
🚇 Passeig de Gràcia
♿ Good
↔ Eixample (► 42–43); Fundació Antoni Tàpies (► 44)
❓ Guided tours of the *Manzana de la Discòrda* and *La Rute del Modernisme* (a tour connecting all the *Modernista* sights in the city) ► 36, Casa Amatller. Includes discounts to many attractions.

Although Casa Milà is now a World Heritage Site, it so shocked Barcelonans when built that they nicknamed it 'La Pedrera' (the Quarry)

🟥 28C5
✉ Carrer Provença 261–265
☎ 93 484 59 00
🕐 Daily 10–7.30. Guided tours: Mon–Fri at 5:30 in English and Catalan and at 6:30 in Spanish
🚇 Diagonal
♿ Good (but not on roof); excellent toilet
💷 Expensive
↔ Eixample (► 42–43); Gracià (► 44–45); Manzana de la Discòrdia (► 36–37); Sagrada Família (► 24–25)
❓ Audio guide available

Did you know?

The Passeig de Gràcia between Carrer d'Aragó and Consell de Cent, containing Casa Amatller, Batlló and Lleó-Morera, is known as the Manzana de la Discòrdia *(Block of Discord), because of the clashing architectural styles.*

Explore the atmospheric lanes of the Ciutat Vella, a world away from the modern city

CIUTAT VELLA ✪✪✪

The tightly packed maze of narrow streets and alleyways of Barcelona's Ciutat Vella (Old City), bordered by the Ramblas, the Ciutadella Park, Plaça Catalunya and the sea, was once enclosed by medieval city walls and, until the massive building boom of the Eixample (➤ 42–43), 150 years ago, comprised the entire city.

At its heart is the Barri Gòtic (Gothic Quarter), one of several clearly identifiable *barris* or districts which make up the Old City. Its roots can be traced back to 15BC, when Roman soldiers established a small settlement called Barcino on a slight hill here called Mons Taber. This remarkable cluster of dark, twisting streets, quiet patios, sun-splashed squares and grand Gothic buildings was built

inside the Roman fortifications, at a time when Barcelona, along with Genoa and Venice, was one of the three most important merchant cities in the Mediterranean and possessed untold riches. Its crowning glory, the Catedral (➤ 16), is surrounded by former residences of the counts of Barcelona and the Kings of Catalonia and Aragón. To the northwest lies Carrer Portaferrissa, the Old City's principal shopping street, with trendy boutiques and shopping arcades. To the south lies the spacious Plaça Sant Jaume (➤ 69) and a cobweb of narrow streets and interconnecting squares, including Plaça Sant Felip Neri, with its fine baroque church, Plaça del Pi, with its market of local produce (➤ 75), and leafy Plaça Sant Josep Oriol, the 'Montmartre of Barcelona', where local artists display their works at weekends and buskers entertain the café crowds. Just off the square, the narrow streets bounded by Carrer Banys Nous, Call and Bisbe once housed a rich Jewish ghetto called *El Call*, but now the area is known for its antique shops.

As the city grew more prosperous in the early Middle Ages, new *barris* developed around the Roman perimeter, including La Mercè to the south and La Ribera to the east. The area south of Carrer de Ferran – La Mercè – is focused around the elegant, arcaded Plaça Reial (➤ 69) and the Church of La Mercè, Barcelona's patron Virgin. Though once very prosperous, this *barri* has become shabby and run-down, but is still worth exploring if only to seek out the excellent locals' *tapas* bars along Carrer de la Mercè.

The *barri* of La Ribera, east of Via Laietana, holds much to interest the visitor. Its name (The Waterfront) recalls the time when the shoreline reached considerably further inland during Barcelona's Golden Age, when it was the city's main centre of commerce and trade and the favourite residential area of the merchant élite. Their handsome Gothic palaces still line its main street, Carrer Montcada. Several have since been converted into museums and galleries including Museu Picasso (➤ 20) and Galeria Maeght (➤ 107). The street leads to Santa Maria del Mar, the 'seaside cathedral' (➤ 26) and the Passeig del Born, with its popular restaurants, bars and craft shops.

Above: tiled detail on a drinking fountain in the Barri Gòtic
Below: look for the ornate balconies and other hidden details above the shop fronts

Barri Gòtic

Distance
2km

Time
1 hour (excluding visits)

Start/end point
Plaça Nova
✚ 41B3
Ⓜ Catalunya, Urquinaona

Coffee break
Mesón del Café (€)
✉ Carrer Llibreteria 16, just off Plaça Sant Jaume I
☎ 93 315 07 54

Leave Plaça Nova via the Portal del Bisbe (part of the Roman wall) into Carrer del Bisbe. Turn first left into Carrer de Santa Llúcia.

Note the tiny chapel of Santa Llúcia to your right, and the Gothic Archdeacon's House (Casa de l'Ardiaca) to your left. Just beyond is the main entrance to the Catedral (➤ 16).

From Plaça de la Seu, follow Carrer dels Comtes beside the cathedral, past Museu Frederic Marès (➤ 55). A left turn into Baixada de Santa Clara leads to Plaça del Rei (➤ 68). Return to the cathedral and skirt round its buttresses past the 14th-century Canon's House (Casa del Cánonges).

Stone plaques on the façade portray twin towers supported by winged goats with lions' feet, the heraldic symbols of medieval Barcelona.

Intricate stone lacework makes this bridge on Carrer del Bisbe unique

Turn sharp left, then left again onto Carrer del Bisbe, under a bridge and into Plaça Sant Jaume (➤ 69). Take Carrer de la Ciutat, then the first left until you reach Plaça Sant Just.

Here, the Església dels Sants Just i Pastor is reputedly the oldest church in Barcelona. Opposite, note the faded frescos on an elegant townhouse.

Leave the square along Carrer del Lledó. Turn first left then left again at the House of the Blue Tiles. Following the line of the Roman wall, cross Carrer Jaume I and continue up Carrer de la Tapineria, once the main street of medieval shoemakers.

Constructed between 270 and 310 AD, Barcelona's Roman walls were outgrown by the 11th century.

Continue along Carrer de la Tapineria past more Roman remains and return to Plaça Nova.

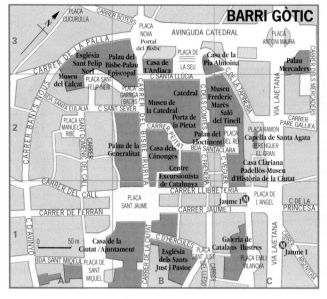

BARRI GÒTIC

DRASSANES AND MUSEU MARÍTIM ●●●

Barcelona's Museu Marítim (Maritime Museum) is located in the magnificent Drassanes Reials (Royal Shipyards), a splendid example of Gothic civil architecture. Since the 13th century, these impressive yards have been dedicated to the construction of ships for the Crowns of Catalonia and Aragon.

Today, their vast, cathedral-like, stone-vaulted halls contain maps, charts, paintings, pleasure craft and a huge range of other seafaring memorabilia chronicling the remarkable maritime history of Barcelona. The most impressive exhibit is a 60m replica of *La Real*, flagship of Don Juan of Austria, which forms part of an exciting 45-minute spectacle – 'The Great Sea Adventure'. Through headphones, visual and acoustic effects, visitors can experience life as a galley slave, encounter a Caribbean storm, join emigrants bound for the New World, and explore the seabed on board *Ictineo*, claimed to be the world's first submarine and built by Catalan inventor Narcís Monturiol.

* 29E3
* Avinguda de les Drassanes s/n
* 93 342 99 20
* Daily 10–7
* Café-restaurant (€)
* Drassanes
* 14, 18, 36, 38, 57, 59, 64, 91
* Few
* Expensive (free first Sat of each month after 3PM)
* Ciutat Vella (➤ 38–39); Monument a Colom (➤ 50); Port Vell (➤ 72); La Rambla (➤ 23)
* Library, bookshop, gift shop

Life on the ocean wave is explored in the Museu Marítim

L'EIXAMPLE ✪✪

L'Eixample means 'The Extension' in Catalan, and this district was laid out between 1860 and 1920 to expand the city beyond the confines of its medieval walls and to link it with the outlying municipalities of Sants, Sarrià-Sant Gervasi and Gràcia.

The innovative plan, drawn up by liberal-minded civil engineer Ildefons Cerdà, broke completely with the tradition of Spanish urban planning, with its geometric grid of streets running parallel to the seafront, neatly dividing an area of 9sq km into 550 symmetrical blocks. The aptly named Avinguda Diagonal cuts through the rectilinear blocks at 45° to add a touch of originality. The utopian features of Cerdà's plan – such as gardens in the middle of each block and buildings on only two sides – have been largely forgotten, and today many people scorn the district for its monotony while others praise it as a visionary example of urban planning.

The Eixample is divided into two *barris*, either side of Carrer Balmes. *L'Esquerra* (The Left) is largely residential and of less interest to visitors, whereas *La Dreta* (The Right) contains many of Barcelona's greatest *Modernistame* landmarks, including Casa Milà, the three properties of La Manzana de la Discòrdia, the Fundació Antoni Tàpies, the Hospital de la Santa Creu i Sant Pau, and the Sagrada Família. It is also a district of offices, banks and hotels. Chic boutiques and shops line its streets and, at night, Barcelona's smart set frequents its many restaurants, designer bars and discos.

Above: *Passeig de Gràcia, with its many shops, bars and restaurants, is one of the city's liveliest streets*

WALK

The Eixample District

This walk explores some of Barcelona's lesser-known examples of *Modernista* architecture.

Start in Plaça de Catalunya, and walk up Passeig de Gràcia.

This elegant avenue has its original wrought-iron street lamps with ceramic mosaic seats dating from 1906. Note Nos 6–14 (one of the last *Modernista* constructions), No 18 (the only surviving example of rationalist commercial architecture in Barcelona) and No 21.

Turn left at Casa Lleó-Morera (► 37), along Carrer Consell de Cent then first left into Rambla de Catalunya, past several contrasting Modernista buildings (Nos 47, 54 and 77) until Diagonal. Turn right past Gaudí-influenced Casa Comalat at No 442 by Salvador Valery and continue until Puigi Cadafalch's Palau Quadras at No 373.

This striking neo-Gothic building contains the Museu de la Música. Near by, UNESCO-listed Casa Terrades (Nos 416–20) is sometimes known as Casa de les Punxes ('House of Spikes') because of its steep gables and red-tiled turrets.

Turn right into Carrer Roger de Lluria, past Palau Montaner (Carrer Mallorca 278), an early work by Domènech i Montaner, and turn left into Carrer València, past Nos 285, 293, and 312, striking Modernista buildings, and a large enclosed market. At Avinguda Diagonal, turn right.

Don't miss the extraordinary undulating wooden façade of Casa Planells (No 332), by one of Gaudí's early collaborators, Josep Maria Jujol.

Turn left into Carrer Sicilia and continue on to the Sagrada Família (► 24–25).

Distance
4km

Time
2–2½ hours (excluding visits)

Start point
Plaça de Catalunya
🚇 29D4
Ⓜ Catalunya

End point
Sagrada Família
🚇 29E6
Ⓜ Sagrada Família

Lunch break
Buy a picnic in the large, covered market (Mercat de la Concepció) to eat in Plaça Sagrada Família.
✉ Mercat de la Concepció, Carrer València

Above: *Casa Josefa Villanueva in Carrer València – one of the many* Modernista *buildings in the Eixample*

43

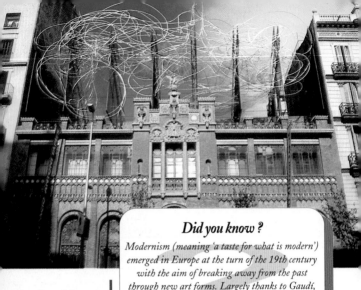

Did you know ?

*Modernism (meaning 'a taste for what is modern')
emerged in Europe at the turn of the 19th century
with the aim of breaking away from the past
through new art forms. Largely thanks to Gaudí,
Catalan Modernisme had the biggest impact,
influencing all forms of European art, architecture,
literature, and theatre, and making Barcelona an
open-air museum of Modernism.*

*Extraordinary skyline –
Fundació Tàpies' Cloud
and Chair sculpture*

🔲 29D5
✉ Carrer d'Aragó 255
☎ 93 487 03 15
🕐 Tue–Sun 10–8. Closed
Mon
🚌 7, 16, 17, 20, 22, 24, 28,
43, 44
🚇 Passeig de Gràcia
♿ Good
💷 Moderate, children under
16 free
🔳 Manzana de la Discòrdia
(➤ 36–37, and panel)
❓ Library and small
bookshop

FUNDACIÓ ANTONI TÀPIES ✪

The Tàpies Foundation was founded by Catalan artist
Antoni Tàpies in 1984 to promote the study and under-
standing of modern art. It is housed in the former
Montaner i Simon publishing house, built by Lluís
Domènech i Montaner between 1880 and 1889, an
unusual building that is considered the initiator of the
Modernist movement. The striking *Mudejar*-style façade is
crowned by an eye-catching tangle of wire and tubing by
Tàpies, entitled *Cloud and Chair* (1990). Inside, there is an
exhaustive library documenting art and artists of the 20th
century, and one of the most complete collections of
Tàpies' own works.

FUNDACIÓ JOAN MIRÓ (➤ 17, TOP TEN)

🔲 28C6
🍴 Plenty (€–€€€)
🚇 Fontana, Gràcia, Joanic,
Plaça Molina
❓ Festa Major every August
(➤ 116)

GRÀCIA ✪

In 1820, Gràcia was a mere village of about 2,500 inhabitants. By 1897, the population had swollen to 61,000,
making it the ninth-largest city in Spain, known as a radical
centre of Catalanism and anarchism, still reflected in some
street names – Mercat de la Llibertat and Plaça de la
Revolució. Since then, Gràcia has been engulfed by the
expanding metropolis, yet even now it maintains a village-
like, no-frills, bohemian atmosphere and the *Graciencs* still
call the cityfolk *Barcelonins*.

There are no real 'tourist' attractions here, except Gaudí's first major commission, Casa Vicens (✉ Carrer de les Carolines 24). Gràcia's real appeal is its muddle of narrow atmospheric streets and squares, and a concentration of reasonably priced bars, restaurants and popular night venues.

HOSPITAL DE LA SANTA CREU I SANT PAU ★★

This remarkable hospital complex is a masterpiece of *Modernisme* by innovative architect Lluís Domènech i Montaner. Not only did he deliberately defy the orderliness of the Eixample by aligning the buildings at 45 degrees to the street grid, but he also built the complex in contradiction to established hospital concepts by creating a 'hospital-village' of 48 small pavilions connected by underground passages and surrounded by gardens, rather than one single massive building.

Construction began in 1902, as a long-overdue replacement for the old hospital in the Raval, following a bequest from a Catalan banker called Pau Gil. The new hospital was inaugurated in 1930. The main pavilion, with its graceful tower and ornate mosaic façade, serves as a majestic entrance to the whole ensemble. Inside, the various pavilions are grouped around gardens that occupy an area equivalent to nine blocks of the Eixample, where both doctors and patients alike can enjoy a peaceful natural environment. The pavilions are decorated in ornate *Modernista* style using brick, colourful ceramics and natural stone. Over the years, the hospital complex has been restored several times and in 1984 it was declared a World Cultural Heritage site by UNESCO.

➕ 62A4
✉ Carrer de Sant Antoni Maria Claret 167–71
☎ 93 488 20 78
🕐 Guided tours every half hour Sat–Sun 10–2
🍴 Small coffee shop in one of the pavilions (€)
🚇 Hospital de Sant Pau
💰 Moderate; grounds free
↔ Gràcia (➤ 44); Parc Güell (➤ 21); Sagrada Família (➤ 24–25)
❓ Please remember that this is a hospital and not a tourist attraction

The main hospital of the Eixample – more palatial than most!

SANT FELÍU
DE LLOBREGAT

5

AUTOPISTA ZARAGOZA

VALLVIDRERA

Funicular
de Vallvidrera

Museu Verdaguer

SANT JUST
DESVERN

S e r r a   d e

SARRIA-SANT GERVASI

ESPLUGUES
DE LLOBREGAT

4

CARRETERA D'ESPLUGUES

RONDA DE DALT

CARRER DE COLLBLANC

Museu Monestir de
Pedralbes/Collecció
PEDRALBES Thyssen-Bornemisza

Palau Reial
de Pedralbes

RONDA

LES CORTS
Area Diagonal

AVINGUDA DIAGONAL

Museu del Futbol
Club Barcelona/
Camp Nou

CARRER DE CARLOS III

Jardins Poeta
Eduard Marquina

L'HOSPITALET
DE LLOBREGAT

SANTS

3

Tarragona

CARRER DE SANTS

Estació Barcelona
Central-Sants

GRAN VIA DE SANTS

Parc de l'Espanya
Industrial

Hospi

AVINGUDA DE LA GRANVIA

Aeropuerto
de Barcelona

Hostafrancs

Parc de
Joan Miró

GRAN VIA DE LES CORTS CATALANES

PASSEIG DE LA ZONA FRANCA

Poble Espanyol

Palau Nacional

POBLE
SEC

EL RAVA

2

Sants-Montjuïc

Fundació Joan Miró

CINTURÓ DEL LITORAL

Muntanya
de Montjuïc

Estadi Olímpic

Muse
Maríi

ZONA FRANCA-PORT

Castell de Montjuïc

RONDA LITORAL

1

Llobregat

A   B   C

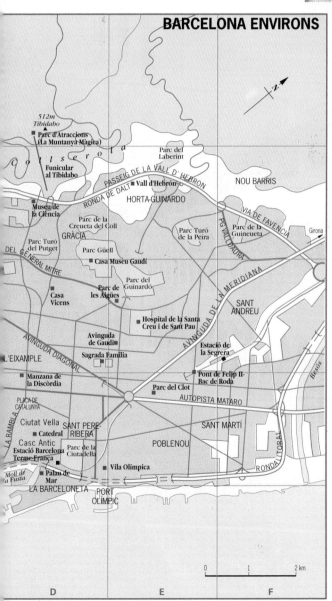

BARCELONA ENVIRONS

512m
Tibidabo ▲

■ Parc d'Atraccions
(La Muntanya Màgica)

o l l s e r o l a

Parc del
Laberint

NOU BARRIS

Funicular
al Tibidabo

PASSEIG DE LA VALL D'HEBRON

RONDA DE DALT

■ Vall d'Hebrón

VIA DE FAVENCIA

■ Museu de
la Ciència

HORTA-GUINARDO

Girona

Parc de la
Creueta del Coll

Parc Turó
de la Peira

Parc de la
Guineueta

GRÀCIA

Parc Güell

PG VALLDAURA

Parc Turó
del Putget

DEL GENERAL MITRE

■ Casa Museu Gaudí

Parc del
Guinardó

AVINGUDA DE LA MERIDIANA

SANT
ANDREU

■ Casa
Vicens

Parc de
les Aigües ■

■ Hospital de la Santa
Creu i de Sant Pau

AVINGUDA DIAGONAL

Avinguda
de Gaudí ■

L'EIXAMPLE

Sagrada Família ■

Estació de
la Segrera ■

Besòs

■ Manzana de
la Discòrdia

■ Pont de Felip II-
Bac de Roda

PLAÇA DE
CATALUNYA

Parc del Clot ■

AUTOPISTA MATARO

Ciutat Vella

SANT PERE-

SANT MARTÍ

LA RAMBLA

■ Catedral

RIBERA

POBLENOU

Casc Antic

Parc de la
Ciutadella

Estació Barcelona
Terme-França

RONDA LITORAL

Moll de
la Fusta

■ Palau de
Mar

■ Vila Olímpica

LA BARCELONETA

PORT
OLÍMPIC

0   1   2 km

D   E   F

MERCAT DE LA BOQUERIA ✪✪

Of more than 40 food markets in Barcelona, La Boqueria is the best and the busiest – always bustling with local shoppers, restaurateurs, gourmands and tourists. Its cavernous market hall (best entered through an imposing wrought-iron entranceway halfway up La Rambla) was built in the 1830s to house the food stalls that cluttered La Rambla and surrounding streets.

Inside is a riot of noise, perfumes and colours, with a myriad stalls offering all the specialities of the Mediterranean and the Catalonian hinterland – mouth-watering displays of fruit and vegetables, a glistening array of exotic fish, endless strings of sausages and haunches of ham, and sweetly scented bunches of herbs.

✚ 62A3
✉ Rambla 91
☎ 93 318 25 84
🕐 Mon–Sat 8AM–8PM. Closed Sun & hols
🍴 Snack bars (€)
Ⓜ Liceu
♿ Few
⚟ Free
↔ Ciutat Vella (➤ 38–39); Drassanes and Museu Marítim (➤ 41); Plaça Reial (➤ 69); La Rambla (➤ 23); Gran Teatre del Liceu (➤ 114)

MONESTIR DE PEDRALBES AND COLLECCIÓ THYSSEN-BORNEMISZA ✪✪

The monastery of Pedralbes was founded by King Jaume II and Queen Elisenda de Montcada in 1326 to accommodate nuns of the St Clare of Assisi order. Following the king's death in 1327, Elisenda spent the last 37 years of her life here.

The spacious, three-storey cloisters – one of the architectural jewels of Barcelona – are still used by the Clarista nuns. Step inside and it is hard to believe you are just a short bus ride from frenetic downtown Barcelona. From here, there is access to the refectory, the chapter house, the Queen's grave and St Michael's cell, with its remarkable wall murals.

Recently, Baron von Thyssen-Bornemisza donated part of his priceless art collection to the monastery, with 79 works housed in two former dormitories – mostly 13th- to 18th-century Italian and German paintings, including works by Fra Angélico, Lucas Cranach, Velázquez and Rubens .

✚ 46C4
✉ Baixada de Monestir 9
☎ Monastery: 93 203 92 82. Thyssen-Bornemisza Collection: 93 280 14 34
🕐 Monastery and museums: Tue–Sun 10–2. Closed Mon and hols. Church: Tue–Sun 11–1
🚌 22, 63, 64, 75
♿ Excellent
⚟ Monastery: moderate. Thyssen-Bornemisza: moderate
↔ Palau Reial de Pedralbes (➤ 61)
❓ Bookshop, gift shop

MONTJUÏC (➤ 18, TOP TEN)

Left: *the lively, colourful Mercat de la Boqueria*
Opposite: *enjoy a peaceful stroll through the Monestir de Pedralbes*

✚ 62A1
✉ Plaça Portal de la Pau
☎ 93 302 52 24
🕐 Daily Oct–May 10–6:30,
Jun–Sep 9–8:30. Closed
hols
🚇 Drassanes
💷 Cheap
↔ Port Vell (➤ 72)

MONUMENT A COLOM ✪

This vast monument, commemorating the return of Christopher Columbus to Barcelona in 1493 from his first trip to the Americas, stands outside the naval headquarters of Catalonia, at the seaward end of the Ramblas. It was designed by Gaietà Buigas for the Universal Exposition of 1888, with Columbus standing at the top of a 50m column, pointing out to sea – towards Italy! Take the lift to the top for breathtaking bird's-eye views of the harbourfront.

MUSEU D'ART CONTEMPORANI DE ✪✪
BARCELONA (MACBA)

The new Barcelona Museum of Contemporary Art (MACBA), inaugurated in 1995, focuses on the art movements of the second half of the 20th century.

The museum building, itself a work of art designed by the American architect Richard Meier, has been the subject of much controversy but is increasingly being included as one of Barcelona's must-see landmarks. The vast white edifice with swooping ramps and glass-walled galleries almost upstages the works on display. Its location – surrounded by shabby old houses in the rundown district of Raval – is intended to spearhead investment in the neighbourhood.

MACBA's extensive collection (exhibited in rotation) covers the 1940s to the 1990s, with special emphasis on Catalan and Spanish artists. It contains works by Klee, Miró and Tàpies, along with many others, including Joan Brossa, Maurizio Cattelan and Damien Hirst.

✚ 62A5
✉ Plaça dels Àngels 1
☎ 93 412 08 10
🕐 Mon–Fri 11–7:30, Sat
10–8, Sun and hols 10–3.
Longer opening hours in
summer. Guided tours
Wed & Sat 6PM, Sun &
hols 12 noon
🍴 Café (€)
🚇 Catalunya, Universitat
♿ Excellent
💷 Expensive
↔ Ciutat Vella (➤ 38–39);
La Rambla (➤ 23)

Above: *the Monument a Colom makes an impressive sight*

50

La Rambla

Start at Plaça Portal de la Pau, with your back to the sea and La Colom Monument (➤ 50), and head up the Ramblas, beginning at La Rambla de Santa Mònica. The convent here is the only 17th-century building still standing on La Rambla.

This first section of Barcelona's famous street can be dangerous, especially at night, as it borders the Barri Xinès (China Town) district, renowned as a centre of drugs and crime. If you visit El Ravel after dark, take a taxi.

Continue up to Plaça del Teatre and the Rambla dels Caputxins, on the site of an ancient Capuchin convent.

This was once the heart of the old theatre district, marked by a statue of Serafi Pitarra, 'father' of contemporary theatre in Catalonia. Today, only the shabby Teatro Principal remains.

Continue north past the Gran Teatre del Liceu (➤ 114) to Rambla de Sant Josep, which begins where the street widens, at Mercat de la Boqueria (➤ 49).

A meat market used to be held in the Plaça de la Boqueria. Indeed, 'boqueria' means 'butcher'. Today the square is decorated with a mosaic by Joan Miró. Flower-stands line this section, commonly called the Rambla de les Flors, whereas birds and other small creatures are sold in the Rambla dels Estudis, named after a university which once stood here, although now dubbed the Rambla dels Ocells (Boulevard of the Birds).

The final Rambla – La Rambla de Canaletes, named after its famous fountain (➤ 23) – leads to Plaça de Catalunya, the square where the city's heart beats fastest (➤ 67).

You can frequently find street artists in the Rambla dels Caputxins

Distance
1km

Time
1 hour

Start point
Plaça Portal de la Pau
🚹 62A1
Ⓜ Drassanes

End point
Plaça de Catalunya
🚹 62B5
Ⓜ Catalunya

Coffee break
Café de l'Òpera (➤ 98)
✉ Rambla dels Caputxins 74
☎ 93 302 41 80

51

Food & Drink

No one visiting Barcelona should leave without trying *la cuina Catalana*, its cuisine, described by the American food critic Colman Andrews as 'the last great culinary secret in Europe'. Rooted in the fresh local ingredients of the mountains, the plains and sea, the food is delicious and suprisingly subtle in flavour.

Mediterranean Flavours

The main ingredients of traditional Catalan dishes are typically Mediterranean: tomatoes, garlic, olive oil, aubergines, courgettes, peppers and herbs, which, when blended, form *samfaina*, a delicious sauce served with many dishes. Other principal sauces include *picada* (nuts, bread, parsley, garlic and saffron), *sofregit* (a simple sauce of onion, tomato and garlic lightly fried in olive oil) and *allioli* (a strong, garlicky mayonnaise).

For centuries pork (*llom*) has been the cornerstone of the Catalan diet. Little is wasted – even the *peus de porc* (pigs' trotters) are considered a delicacy. No bar would be complete without its haunch of *permil* (cured ham), a popular *tapas* dish (▶ 95 panel), and you often see a variety of sausages hanging from the rafters of restaurants and delicatessens. Lamb, chicken, duck, beef and game also feature strongly, often prepared *a la brasa* (on an open charcoal grill) and served with lashings of *allioli*.

Fresh fish is one of the gourmet delights of la Cuina Catalana

Mar i Muntanya

In Catalan cuisine, meat is commonly combined with fruit, creating such mouth-watering dishes as *pollastre amb pera* (chicken with pears) and *conill amb prunes* (rabbit with prunes). However, it is the unique 'surf'n'turf' combinations that sea and mountain (*Mar i Muntanya*) produce which differentiate *la cuina Catalana* from the cookery of other Spanish regions. *Sípia amb mandonguilles* (cuttlefish with meatballs) and *mar i cel* ('sea and heaven' – made with sausages, rabbit, shrimp and fish) are especially tasty.

Near the coast, fish dishes reign supreme, ranging from simple grilled *sardinas* (sardines) and hearty *sarsuela* (seafood stew) to eye-catching shellfish displays. Try *suquet de peix* (fish and potato soup) or the more unusual *broudegos* ('dog soup') made with fresh fish, onions and orange juice, followed by speciality dishes *arròs negre* (rice cooked in black squid ink), *fideuà* (a local variant of paella, using pasta and not rice) or *bacallà* (salt cod), which comes *a la llauna* (with garlic, parsley, tomato and white wine), *esqueixada* (in an onion, olive and tomato salad), *amb samfaina* or *amb romesco* (a piquant sauce, made from a mixture of crushed nuts, tomatoes and spicy red pepper).

Fine Wines

A short distance south of Barcelona, the Penedès is the main Catalan wine region, producing red (*negre*), white (*blanc*) and rosé (*rosat*) wines. Look for the reliable Torres, Masia Bach and René Barbier labels. Catalan *cava* (sparkling wine) also comes from the Penedès wineries, made by the *méthode champenoise* (➤ 113 panel). Famous names include Freixenet and Codorníu, which can be sampled in the champagne bars of Barcelona. To the north, the Alella and Empordà regions produce white wines, while Priorat produces excellent, heavy reds.

Visitors with a sweet tooth also find sustenance in Barcelona (➤ 96 panel)

Tasty tapas; tucking into portions of prawns and snails

➕ 28C2
✉ Palau Nacional, Parc de
Montjuïc
☎ 93 622 03 76
🕐 Tue–Sat 10–7; Sun and
hols 10–2:30. Closed
Mon
🍴 Café-bar (€)
Ⓜ Espanya
🚌 9, 13, 30, 50, 55
♿ Excellent
💰 Expensive; free first Thu
of month
↔ Anella Olímpica (➤ 32)

MUSEU D'ART MODERN – MNAC ★★

The Museum of Modern Art moved from the imposing
Palau de la Ciutadella, in the Parc de la Ciutadella, in 2004
to join other major collections in the National Museum of
Catalan Art (➤ 19) where it completes a period spanning
the 11th to 20th centuries devoted to Catalan art from the
mid-19th century to around 1930.

The collection starts with works by Maria Fortuny, the
earliest of the *Modernistas* and the first Catalan artist to
be known widely abroad, and friends Ramon Casas,
whose work once hung on the walls of Els Quatre Gats
(➤ 94), and Santiago Rusinyol. However, the highlight of
the museum is, without doubt, its decorative arts
collection: jewellery, textiles, stained glass, ironwork,

sculptures, ceramics and painted screens by Homar, Puig l Cadafalch and Gaudí, among others.

The extravagance of *Modernisme* was succeeded by the less adventurous *Noucentisme* movement, which attempted to reintroduce the more harmonious values of Classical and Mediterranean art, epitomised by the works of Casanovas and Sunyer. The fascinating exhibition draws to a close with a series of striking avant-garde sculptures by Gargallo and Juli González, dating from the 1920s and 30s.

MUSEU FREDERIC MARÈS ✪

Entrance to this museum, founded by local sculptor Frederic Marès in 1946, is via a beautiful medieval courtyard, which was once part of the Royal Palace of the Kings and Queens of Catalonia and Aragon. The museum itself is divided into two main sections: the sculpture collection, featuring works from the pre-Roman period to the 20th century, and the 'Sentimental Museum', which portrays daily life from the 15th to 20th centuries through an astonishing assortment of household items. Highlights include the women's section (with collections of fans, parasols, hat pins and jewellery), the smoker's room, and the charming entertainments room, with its puppet theatres, wind-up toys and dolls.

Left: *Religious imagery in the Museu Frederic Marès*

🕂 62C3
✉ Plaça de Sant Iu 5–6
☎ 93 310 58 00
🕐 Tue–Sat 10–7, Sun 10–3, closed hols
🍴 Summer café (€)
🚇 Jaume I
♿ Few
🎫 Moderate. Free 1st Sun of month and every Wed PM
↔ Catedral (▶ 16); Ciutat Vella (▶ 38–39); Museu d'Història de la Ciutat (▶ 56); Plaça del Rei (▶ 68); Plaça Sant Jaume (▶ 69)
❓ Library, shop, guided visits

Did you know?

FC Barcelona, or Barça for short, is more than Spain's top football club, the fifth most successful business in Spain, and the richest sports club in the world. During the Franco era, it stood as a Catalan symbol around which people could rally, and this emotional identification still remains today. It also explains why this legendary club has the world's largest soccer club membership (over 100,000 members) and why the streets still erupt with ecstatic revellers following a win over arch-rivals, Real Madrid.

MUSEU DEL FUTBOL CLUB BARCELONA ✪✪

If you can't get a ticket to see Europe's top football team in action, then at least visit the Barcelona Football Club Museum, the city's most visited museum after the revered Picasso Museum (▶ 20). Even those who loathe football can't help marvelling at the vast Nou Camp stadium, which seats over 98,000 spectators. The museum, under the terraces, presents a triumphant array of trophies, photographs and replays of highlights in the club's history before leading you to the shop, where everyone can buy a club shirt, pen, scarf, badge, mug…

🕂 46B3
✉ Nou Camp – Entrance 7 or 9, Carrer Arístides Maillol
☎ 93 496 36 00
🕐 Mon–Sat 10–6, Sun10–2, closed hols
🍴 Café (€)
🚇 Collblanc, Maria Cristina
🎫 Moderate. ♿ Good
❓ Gift shop

+ 62C3
✉ Plaça del Rei s/n
☎ 93 315 11 11
🕐 Tue–Sat 10–2, 4–8,
(Jul–Sep 10–8), Sun and
hols 10–2.
🚇 Jaume I, Liceu
♿ Few
💵 Moderate (free 1st Sat
afternoon of the month)
🔗 Catedral (➤ 16); Ciutat
Vella (➤ 38–39); Museu
Frederic Marès (➤ 55);
Plaça Sant Jaume (➤ 69)
❓ Information service, shop
and guided tours

Above: *the entrance of
the Museu d'Història de
la Ciutat*

+ 35E5
✉ Gran Via de les Corts
Catalanes 749
☎ 93 245 58 03
🕐 Apr–Sep Mon–Sat 11–2,
4–8; Sun 11–1
🚇 Monumental
💵 Moderate

MUSEU D'HISTÒRIA DE LA CIUTAT ✪✪✪

The Museu d'Història de la Ciutat (City History Museum) is responsible for researching, conserving and publicising Barcelona's heritage. It is split into several sections in various locations around the Plaça del Rei (➤ 68). To start, visitors can familiarise themselves with the earliest origins of the city by wandering around the underground walkways beneath the square, which explore a vast area of excavations that have exposed the ancient Roman settlement of Barcino.

The main entrance to the museum complex is at the opposite end of the square, in Casa Padellàs, a medieval mansion which was moved here stone by stone when the Via Laietana was created in 1930. Inside, carefully chosen, thoroughly documented exhibits trace Barcelona's remarkable evolution through two thousand years of history from a Roman trading-post to a wealthy 18th-century metropolis. Climb to the lookout point high above the galleries for memorable views of the square and the old city.

Back in the square, a visit to the medieval buildings of the Palau Reial Major (the Great Royal Palace ➤ 68), completes the tour of the museum.

MUSEU NACIONAL D'ART DE CATALUNYA (➤ 19, TOP TEN)

MUSEU PICASSO (➤ 20, TOP TEN)

MUSEU TAURI DE LA MONUMENTAL ✪

Even though bullfighting has never had a particularly passionate following in Catalonia, the Museu Tauri De La Monumental (Bullfighting Museum), located inside the Monumental Bullring, is undoubtedly one of Barcelona's more unusual museums, with its dazzling array of fancy capes and costumes, photographs, old bullfighting posters and the mounted heads of bulls.

MUSEU TÈXTIL I D'INDUMENTÀRIA ⭐

The Museu Tèxtil i d'Indumentària (Textile and Clothing Museum) acts as a reminder of how, thanks to its thriving textile industry, Barcelona rose to prosperity in the 1800s. It occupies a beautiful 14th-century palace, in what would then have been the aristocratic heart of Barcelona.

The museum collections include textiles, tapestries, lace and clothes from medieval to modern times, with displays of textile machinery, dolls, shoes, and other fashion accessories.

- 🕂 63D2
- ✉ Carrer Montcada 12–14
- ☎ 93 319 76 03
- 🕐 Tue–Sat 10–6, Sun and hols 10–3. Closed Mon
- 🍴 Café–restaurant (€)
- Ⓜ Jaume I
- ♿ Good
- 💷 Moderate
- ↔ Museu Picasso (➤ 20)

PALAU GÜELL ⭐⭐⭐

This extraordinary building, constructed in 1886–88 and declared a World Cultural Heritage site by UNESCO, was Antoni Gaudí's first major architectural project, commissioned by the Güell family.

The façade is particularly striking, with its twin arches leading into the central vestibule. Off the latter are various rooms decorated with *Modernista* fittings. A ramp leads down to the basement stables, constructed with bare-brick columns and arches. The rooftop terrace is a mixture of random spires, battlements and chimneys of differing shapes and sizes, decorated with coloured ceramic mosaics. Look closely and on one you will find a reproduction of Cobi, the 1992 Barcelona Olympics mascot.

Unfortunately, the Güell family did not live here long. In 1936, the palace was confiscated by Spanish Civil War anarchists, who used it as their military headquarters and prison.

- 🕂 29D3
- ✉ Carrer Nou de la Rambla 3–5
- ☎ 93 317 39 74
- 🕐 Mon–Sat 10–6:15. Closed Sun & hols
- Ⓜ Liceu
- ♿ None
- 💷 Cheap. Guided tours only starting every 15 minutes and lasting one hour
- ↔ Mercat de la Boqueria (➤ 49); Ciutat Vella (➤ 38–39); Plaça Reial (➤ 69); La Rambla (➤ 23)

Plaça de Toros Monumental – Barcelona's main bullring

- 47D2
- Plaça Pau Vila 3, Port Vell
- 93 225 47 00
- Tue–Sat 10–7, Wed 10–8, Sun and hols 10–2:30
- Rooftop café (€)
- Barceloneta
- Excellent
- Moderate (free 1st Sun of month)
- Barceloneta (➤ 33); Museu Picasso (➤ 20); Museu Tèxtil i d'Indumentària (➤ 57); Port Vell (➤ 72); Santa Maria del Mar (➤ 26)
- Gift shop, multimedia library, community programmes

The newly renovated Palau de Mar warehouse is renowned for its excellent seafood restaurants

PALAU DE MAR ✪✪✪

Thanks to the influence of the Olympic Games, and the opening up of the old port as a leisure area, the Palau de Mar (Palace of the Sea) – an impressive late 19th-century warehouse – has recently been converted into offices, harbourside restaurants and the spectacular Museu d'Història de Catalunya (Museum of Catalan History).

This is one of Barcelona's most sophisticated museums, opened in 1996. Some critics have dubbed it a 'theme park', because of its lack of original exhibits, but it is nevertheless a dynamic and stimulating museum, covering the history of Catalonia in an entertaining fashion, through state-of-the-art displays, films, special effects, interactive screens and hands-on exhibits – tread an Arab waterwheel, mount a cavalier's charger, drive an early tram, take cover in a Civil War air-raid shelter...

The museum is divided into eight sections, each presenting a thorough picture of the economy, politics, technology, culture and everyday life of Catalonia over the centuries: the region's prehistory, the consolidation of Catalonia in the Middle Ages, its maritime role, links with the Austrian Empire in the 16th and 17th centuries, its economic growth and industrialisation, the 1936 Civil War and the ensuing repression of Catalonia under Franco, through to the restoration of democracy in 1979. The insight this innovative museum provides makes it easier for the visitor to understand the complexities of this 'nation within a nation'.

PALAU DE LA MÚSICA CATALANA ✪✪✪

In a city bursting with architectural wonders, the Palau de la Música Catalana (Palace of Catalan Music) – commissioned by the Orfeó Català (Catalan Musical Society) in 1904 and created by local architect Lluís Domènech i Montaner between 1905 and 1908 – stands out as one of Barcelona's greatest Modernist masterpieces and a symbol of the renaissance of Catalan culture.

The bare brick façade is highlighted with colourful ceramic pillars, fancy windows and busts of Palestrina, Bach, Beethoven and Wagner. The sculptural group projecting from the corner of the building symbolises popular song. A balcony runs around the building and the main structure is supported by ornate columns that form huge dramatic archways over the entrance.

The interior continues the ornamental theme with a profusion of decoration in the entrance hall, foyer and staircase – almost overpowering in its attention to detail. The *pièce de résistance*, however, must be the concert hall, with its exquisite roof (an inverted cupola made of stained glass), its sculptures, ceramics and paintings dedicated to musical muses (including Josep Anselm Clavé, the great 19th-century reviver of Catalan music), and its beautiful balconies and columns, designed to enhance the perspective of the auditorium.

It's no surprise that this is one of the city's main venues for classical music, and, until the restoration of the Liceu Opera House and the opening of the Auditorium, was home to two orchestras, the Liceu and the Orquestra Simfònica de Barcelona i Nacional de Catalunya. It's a memorable experience to attend one of the weekly concerts; the acoustics are as fine as the surroundings.

✚ 63D4
✉ Carrer Sant Francesc de Paula 2
☎ 93 295 72 00
🕐 Daily 10–3:30
🚇 Jaume 1, Urquinaona
♿ Few
💷 Moderate
❓ Guided tours. Early booking for concerts essential

The Palau de la Música Catalana is a feast for the eyes as well as the ears

The Pedralbes District

Distance
3km

Time
1 hour (excluding visits)

Start point
Palau Reial de Pedralbes
🚇 46C4
🚇 Palau Reial

End point
Monestir de Pedralbes
🚇 46C4
🚌 22, 63, 64, 75, 78

The cool cloisters of Monestir de Pedralbes provide some welcome shade from the midday sun

Start at the Palau Reial de Pedralbes (▶ 61). Walk eastwards along the Avinguda de la Diagonal past the Law School and turn left up Avinguda de Pedralbes.

After a short distance on the left is the former Güell Estate (No 15). Note Gaudí's extraordinary wrought-iron entrance gate, which represents a dragon. Today the buildings house La Càtedra Gaudí, an institution specialising in subjects connected with this famous architect.

Continue up Avinguda de Pedralbes until the T-junction. Branch left into Carretera d'Esplugues.

At No 103, the Church of Montserrat was commissioned in 1920 as a gift for the Monastery of Montserrat (▶ 83) for use as a monastic foundation. The bequest was refused, so the property became part of the bishopric of Barcelona in the 1960s.

Turn right in front of the church, up Carrer Abadessa Olzet, left along Avinguda Pearson then right again up Carrer Miret i Sans as far as Carrer de Panama 21.

Here, near the corner (No 21), a charming medieval farmhouse underlines the former rural character of Pedralbes. By contrast, No 13, a magnificent *Modernista* mansion with a gleaming polychromatic tiled roof, reflects the wealth of this district.

The road turns into Carrer de Montevideo and passes behind the monastery of Pedralbes (▶ 49), hidden behind bougainvillaea-smothered walls and framed by the hills of Tibidabo beyond. A flight of steps leads down Baixada del Monestir, past a small, leafy square, to the main entrance.

PALAU REIAL DE PEDRALBES ⭐

The Palau Reial de Pedralbes (Royal Palace of Pedralbes) is the result of the conversion in 1919 of the ancient villa of Can Feliu into a residence to accommodate the Spanish Royal family during the International Exhibition of 1929. After 1939, it became Franco's residence on visits to the city and, after various subsequent uses by royalty and heads of state, was opened to the public in 1960. The geometric gardens were landscaped by Nicolau Rubió i Turdurí, who integrated the existing trees into his design, and there is even a fountain by Gaudí.

Today the state rooms house two museums. The Museu de Ceràmica traces the development of Spanish ceramics from the 12th century onwards, and includes the 18th-century Catalan panels *La Cursa de Braus* (the Bullfight) and *La Xocolotada* (The Chocolate Party), together with works by Picasso and Miró. The Museu de les Arts Decoratives has an impressive collection of decorative arts that spans the early Middle Ages to the present day. Special emphasis is placed on 20th-century developments, from decorative *Modernisme* to such movements as Functionalism and Minimalism, which are both totally void of decoration. The exhibits include some unlikely objects such as coffee-grinders, ice trays and even a urinal!

Above: *of all the luxury mansions in Pedralbes, the Palau Reial is the finest*

➕ 46C4
✉ Avinguda de la Diagonal 686
☎ Museu de les Arts Decoratives: 93 280 50 24. Museu de Ceràmica: 93 280 16 21
🕐 Tue–Sun 10–6 (park 10–sunset)
Ⓜ Palau Reial
🚌 7, 33, 67, 68, 74, 75
♿ Museu d'Arts Decoratives: good. Museu de Ceràmica: few
💶 Museums: moderate (free 1st Sun of month). Park: free
❓ Shop, library, guided visits, educational services

Did you know?

The Zona Alta consists of old villages like Pedralbes, Sarriá, Bonanova and Sant Gervasi. In the 19th century, Barcelona's wealthy would spend their summer months here, in magnificent houses with lush gardens. Along with Horta ('market garden') to the east, with its gentrified farmhouses, this is still the home of many upper middle class Barcelonans.

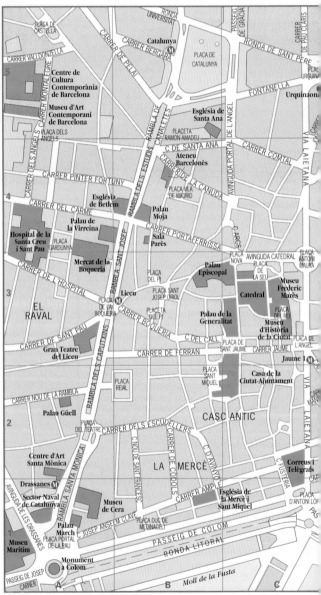

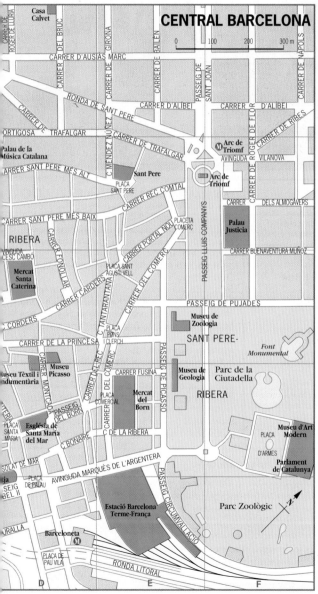

CENTRAL BARCELONA

0   100   200   300 m

Map labels:

CARRER DE ROGER DE LLÚRIA
Casa Calvet
CARRER DEL BRUC
CARRER DE GIRONA
CARRER DE BAILEN
PASSEIG DE SANT JOAN
CARRER DE NÀPOLS

CARRER D'AUSIÀS MARC

RONDA DE SANT PERE
CARRER D'ALIBEI
CARRER DE ROGER DE FLOR
CARRER D'ALIBEI

CARRER DE
ORTIGOSA TRAFALGAR
CARRER DE RIBES
C. MÉNDEZ NÚÑEZ
CARRER DE TRAFALGAR

Palau de la Música Catalana
Arc de Triomf
AVINGUDA VILANOVA

CARRER SANT PERE MÉS ALT
Sant Pere
PLAÇA SANT PERE
Arc de Triomf

CARRER REC COMTAL
CARRER DELS ALMOGAVERS

CARRER SANT PERE MÉS BAIX
PLACETA COMERÇ

RIBERA
CARRER FONOLLAR
CARRER PORTAL NOU
Palau Justicia

AVINGUDA FRANCESC CAMBÓ
CARRER BUENAVENTURA MUÑOZ

PASSEIG LLUÍS COMPANYS

Mercat Santa Caterina
PLAÇA SANT AGUSTÍ VELL
CARRER DEL COMERÇ

CARRER CARDERS
CARRER CARDERS

CARRER CARDERS

C. TANTARANTANA
PASSEIG DE PUJADES

Museu de Zoologia

CORDERS
PLAÇA PONS I CLERCH

CARRER DE LA PRINCESA
SANT PERE-
Font Monumental

Museu de Geologia
Parc de la Ciutadella

Museu Tèxtil i Indumentària
Museu Picasso
CARRER FUSINA
RIBERA

CARRER MONTCADA
CARRER DEL REC
CARRER DEL COMERÇ
PASSEIG DE PICASSO

PLAÇA COMERCIAL
PASSEIG DEL BORN
Mercat del Born
Museu d'Art Modern

PLAÇA SANTA MARIA
Església de Santa Maria del Mar
PLAÇA D'ARMES

C BONAIRE
C DE LA RIBERA
Parlament de Catalunya

CONSOLAT DE MAR
Llotja
PLAÇA DE PALAU
AVINGUDA MARQUÈS DE L'ARGENTERA
PASSEIG CIRCUMVALLACIÓ

PASSEIG ISABEL II

Parc Zoològic

MURALLA
Estació Barcelona Terme-França

Barceloneta

PLAÇA DE PAU VILA
RONDA LITORAL

D   E   F

63

PARC DE LA CIUTADELLA ✪✪

This delightful walled park is a haven of shade and tranquillity just a stone's throw from the old city and waterfront. What's more, hidden among the trees, lawns, promenades and a boating lake, you'll find the Parc Zoológic (➤ 111) and a host of other attractions. This is a great place to relax and people-watch on a pleasant Sunday afternoon.

In 1888 the park was the site of the Universal Exposition and still contains some impressive relics of that great fair, including a striking *Modernista* café which now houses the **Museu de Zoologia**, with highlights that include a fascinating Whale Room and a Sound Library of recordings of animal sounds.

Near by, the neoclassical **Museu de Geologia**, with its rare and valuable minerals, fossils and rocks, opened in 1878 as Barcelona's first public museum. The impressive Hivernacle greenhouse, originally built for the display of exotic plants, is today a popular café (➤ 98), but the main showpiece of the park is the Font Monumental – a huge, neoclassical-style fountain, smothered in allegorical sculptures, which Gaudí contributed to as a student.

Outside the park on Passeig Lluís Companys, the monumental Arc de Triomf was constructed by Josep Vilaseca i Casanovas as the grand entrance to the Universal Exhibition.

Above: the imposing Font Monumental – Niagara meets Brandenburg Gate!

Did you know?

Ciutadella Park takes its name from the mighty citadel constructed here by Felip V, following his victory in the 1714 Siege of Barcelona (➤ 33). The people's hatred of this fortress and their continual protests led to its eventual demolition, and the creation of this large, leafy park in its place, which first opened to the public in 1869.

PARC DEL CLOT

This park in the eastern suburbs has been built on the site of a disused railway yard and combines the walls and arches of the former rail buildings with a low-lying playing-field (the name 'Clot' in Catalan means 'hole') and a shady plaça, linked to a high grassy area of artificial hills and enigmatic sculptures by a lengthy overhead walkway.

PARC DE LA CREUETA DEL COLL

This new park was built in a disused quarry by Olympic architects Martorell and Mackay in 1987. Surrounded by dramatic cliff-faces, scattered with modern sculptures and embracing wooded pathways and a small sand-fringed boating lake, it serves the densely inhabited suburb of Vallcarca and is always packed in summer.

PARC DE L'ESPANYA INDUSTRIAL

With works by many Catalan artists, this is Barcelona's most controversial park – a *nou urbanisme* project, built between 1982 and 1985 on the site of an old textile factory. It is built on two levels, the lower part comprising a large lake and grassy area, with steep white steps up to the much-scorned upper esplanade, where there are ten lighthouses, a series of water spouts and an immense metal play-sculpture entitled the *Dragon of St George*.

PARC GÜELL (► 21, TOP TEN)

47E2
Carrer Escultors Claperós
Nov–Feb 10–6; Mar and Oct 10–7; Apr and Sep 10–8; May–Aug 10–9
Clot, Glories   Free
Sagrada Família
(► 24–25)

47D4
Passeig Mare de Déu del Coll
10–sunset
25, 28, 87
Free
Gràcia (► 44)

28B3
Carrer de Muntadas
Sants-Estació
Free
Montjuïc (► 18); Parc de Joan Miró (► 66)

The Parc de l'Espanya Industrial defies all traditional concepts of park design

Woman and Bird –
centrepiece of Parc de Joan Miró

PARC DE JOAN MIRÓ ⭐

Somewhat rundown these days, but enduringly popular, this park occupies an entire city block on what was formerly the site of a massive abattoir, hence its nickname Parc de l'Escorxador (slaughterhouse). It was created in the 1980s, and is always full of people reading, jogging, dog-walking or playing *petanca* (boules) amid the attractive pergolas and orderly rows of shady palm trees. The park's most famous feature, however, is a startling 22m-high sculpture by Joan Miró, covered in multicoloured ceramic fragments, named *Dona i Ocell* (Woman and Bird).

PARC DEL LABERINT ⭐

These romantic, Italian-style gardens, on the wooded outer rim of Barcelona near the Vall d'Hebrón, present a pleasing contrast to the stark modern *espais urbans* (urban spaces) of the city centre. They originally surrounded a grand 18th-century mansion, which has long since been demolished, but the park has maintained its formal flowerbeds, canals and fountains, its ornamental statuary and its centrepiece – the 'Labyrinth' – a beautiful topiary maze with a statue of Eros at its centre that has given the park its name.

PAVELLÓ MIES VAN DER ROHE ⭐

Bauhaus architect Ludwig Mies van der Rohe created this masterpiece of modern rationalist design for the 1929 Exhibition, a construction of astonishing simplicity and finesse in marble, onyx, glass and chrome, widely acknowledged as one of the classic buildings of the 20th century. It was dismantled at the end of the fair and subsequently meticulously reconstructed and reopened (in its original location) in 1986, on the centenary of Mies van der Rohe's birth.

Inside, take time to enjoy the quality of the colours, textures and materials, as well as a striking bronze sculpture entitled *Der Morgen* (The Morning) and the famous 'Barcelona' chair, a design of timeless elegance created especially for the Expo, which has since been copied worldwide.

PLAÇA DE CATALUNYA ✪

The Plaça de Catalunya is the heart of Barcelona and the hub of the city's transport system. It was first landscaped at the end of the 19th century and soon became of major importance as the pivotal point between the old and new city, with the Barri Gòtic (► 40–41) to the east, the carefully planned new Eixample district (► 42–43) to the north and west, and, to the southeast, La Rambla (► 23) running down to the port.

In 1927 the square was further developed, with the construction of hotels, restaurants and other important buildings. Its main landmarks today are the overpowering head office of Banco Espanol de Crédito, former headquarters of the unified Socialist Party of Catalonia during the Civil War; the monstrous El Corte Inglés department store (► 104, panel); and a medley of fountains and statues, including work by important sculptors such as Gargallo, Marès and Subirachs. Today, its benches, trees and splashing fountains make it a popular place to meet friends and have a coffee or simply to sit and soak up the Mediterranean sun.

🚇 62B5
🍴 Several (€–€€)
Ⓜ Catalunya
↔ Ciutat Vella (► 38–39);
    L'Eixample (► 42–43);
    Palau de la Música
    Catalana (► 59);
    La Rambla (► 23)

Bird's-eye view of Plaça de Catalunya, a popular meeting point at the heart of the city

62C3

Jaume I

Catedral (➤ 16); Ciutat Vella (➤ 38–39); Museu Frederic Marès (➤ 55); Museu d'Història de la Ciutat (➤ 56); Plaça Sant Jaume (➤ 69)

Palau Reial Major

☎ 93 315 11 11

🕐 Palace: Tue–Sat 10–2, 4–8, Sun and hols 10–3 Tower: temporarily closed for restoration

💶 Moderate

❓ Part of the Museu d'Historia de la Ciutat (➤ 56)

The Palau Reial Major and St Marti's tower dominate the Plaça del Rei

PLAÇA DEL REI ✪✪

The charming King's Square was once a bustling medieval marketplace. Today, it forms a frequent backdrop to summer open-air concerts and theatrical events, especially during the Grec festival (➤ 116), and is the location not only of the City History Museum (➤ 56) but also of the **Palau Reial Major** (Great Royal Palace), former residence of the Counts of Barcelona.

It was on the steps leading up to the Palau Reial Major that King Ferdinand and Queen Isabella are said to have received Columbus on his return from his first voyage to America in 1493. Inside, the Spanish Inquisition once sat in the Saló del Tinell, exploiting the local myth that should any prisoner lie, the stones on the ceiling would move. Today, the hall functions as an exhibition area.

On the north side of the square is the chapel of Santa Agata (also part of the royal palace), which contains a precious 15th-century altarpiece by Jaume Huguet. On the opposite side of the square, the Palau de Lloctinent (Palace of the Deputy) was built in 1549 for the Catalan representative of the king in Madrid. The strenuous climb to the top of its five-storey lookout tower (the Mirador del Rei Martí) is well rewarded by sweeping views of the old town.

Did you know?

Catalonia's national folk dance, the sardana, *is performed during summer, either in Plaça Sant Jaume (Sunday, 6–8PM) or in the Plaça de la Seu (Sunday, 10–midday, Wednesday 7–9PM). The dancers are accompanied by an instrumental group* (cobla), *which includes tenor and soprano oboes, a* flabiol *(long flute) and a* tambori *(drum).*

PLAÇA REIAL ✪✪

This sunny porticoed square, just off the Ramblas, with its tall palm trees, decorative fountain and buskers was constructed in 1848. Some of the façades are decorated with terracotta reliefs of navigators and the discoverers of America, and the two tree-like central lampposts mark Gaudí's first commission in Barcelona.

Keep a close watch on your belongings here – the square has a reputation for shady characters and pickpockets, hence the discreet but constant police presence. On Sunday mornings a coin and stamp market is held here.

✚ 62B2
🍴 Plenty (€–€€)
🚇 Liceu or Drassanes
↔ Ciutat Vella (➤ 38–39)

PLAÇA SANT JAUME ✪

Once the hub of Roman Barcelona, this impressive square today represents the city's political heart, and is dominated by two buildings; the neoclassical and Gothic **Casa de la Ciutat** (Town Hall) and, directly opposite, the Renaissance **Palau de la Generalitat de Catalunya** (Government of Catalonia).

The origins of Barcelona's municipal authority date back to 1249, when Jaume I granted the city the right to elect councillors, giving rise to the creation of the Consell de Cent (Council of One Hundred). The famous Saló de Cent (Chamber of One Hundred) and the black marble Saló de las Cronicas (Chamber of the Chronicles) are among the architectural highlights of the Town Hall.

✚ 41B1
🍴 Cafés (€)
🚇 Jaume I
↔ Plaça del Rei (➤ 68), Catedral (➤ 16)

Casa de la Ciutat/Ajuntament
☎ 93 402 70 00
🕐 Sun 10–1:30

Palau de la Generalitat de Catalunya
☎ 93 402 46 00
🕐 Guided tours every 30mins, 10:30AM–1:30PM every 2nd & 4th Sun of each month
🎫 Free

POBLE ESPANYOL (➤ 22, TOP TEN)

Detail on the Palau de la Generalitat in Plaça Sant Jaume

The Waterfront

*Start on Moll de les Drassanes near the
Columbus Monument (▶ 50), then head along
Passeig del Moll de la Fusta by the water's edge.*

Raised on stilts above the yacht basin, the Passeig de
Colom was Barcelona's most stylish promenade when
it opened in 1987, with designer restaurants and bars
and a giant rooftop lobster sculpture (▶ 74). These days
many of the trendier restaurants have closed down and
most of the action has moved to Port Vell (▶ 72) and the
Port Olímpic, but it still makes an interesting scene.

*Continue walking northeast until Plaça
d'Antoni López.*

This busy square is dominated by the main post
office (Correos y Telegrafos) and a notable mosaic
sculpture by Roy Lichtenstein (▶ 74).

Above: *Lichtenstein's
colourful mosaic
sculpture,* Barcelona
Head, *enlivens the
waterfront*
Right: *Barcelona's
waterfront was a stylish
place to be seen in the
heady days of the early
1990s*

Leave the square via the arcaded walkway of Passeig d'Isabel II, past the Stock Exchange and the famous '7 Doors' (Set Portes) restaurant (▶ 95), and turn right at Pla de Palau. Cross the main road into La Barceloneta (▶ 33) and continue along the waterfront, past the Palau de Mar (▶ 58) with its fish restaurants, until you reach Passeig de Joan de Borbó.

Note the wide variety of architectural styles here, especially No 43, which is one of the best examples of 1950s architecture in Barcelona. To your right, the clock tower by the harbour was originally a lighthouse, and the Torre de Sant Sebastià on Moll Nou once carried cable-cars, via the Jaume I Tower, to Montjuïc.

On reaching the seafront, turn left on to Passeig Marítim, which runs parallel to the beach all the way to the Port Olímpic, heralded by a massive, gleaming fish sculpture by Frank Gehry (▶ 33).

Distance
3 km

Time
2–3 hours (excluding visits)

Start point
Monument a Colom
✚ 29E3
Ⓖ Drassanes

End point
Port Olímpic
✚ 47D1
Ⓖ Ciutadella

Lunch break
Emperador (€€€) (▶ 95)
✉ Palau de Mar, Plaça Pau Vila
☎ 93 221 02 20

PORT VELL ⭐⭐

Although Barcelona was founded on sea-going tradition, for many years its seafront was in decay, until a major redevelopment prior to the 1992 Olympics reintegrated the Port Vell (Old Port) into the city by transforming it into a lively new entertainment venue. The Rambla de Mar, a series of undulating wooden walkways and bridges, acts as an extension of La Rambla, connecting the city to Port Vell's many new attractions.

Maremagnum, Port Vell's biggest crowd puller, is a covered shopping and entertainment centre with smart boutiques, expensive restaurants, trendy bars, discos and fast-food joints. Adjacent to the conventional cinema complex, IMAX (► 110), the 'cinema of the future', shows spectacular films in three dimensions, with state-of-the-art wrap-around screens and sound. Near by, the Aquarium (► 110), one of the biggest and best in Europe, always proves popular with children.

Take a **Golondrina** (pleasure boat) for a different perspective of the new harbour developments. The luxurious leisure marina, with over 400 berths, in the previously derelict dockyard area is rapidly becoming one of the Mediterranean's most exclusive anchorages. Although the big ferries to the Balearics still depart from here, most commercial activity now takes place in the modern port further down the coast.

LA RAMBLA (► 23, TOP TEN)

SAGRADA FAMÍLIA (► 24–25, TOP TEN)

SANTA MARIA DEL MAR (► 26, TOP TEN)

Above: *Port Vell Marina – one of the top anchorages of the Mediterranean*

TIBIDABO AND SERRA DE COLLSEROLA ✪✪

The 550m-high Mont Tibidabo forms the northwestern boundary of Barcelona and boasts panoramic views over the entire city, and, on exceptionally clear days, Mallorca.

At its summit, and topped by a huge statue of Christ, stands the modern Church of the Sacred Heart (Sagrat Cor), whose style is probably best described as 'neo-Gothic fantasy'. Near by, the 'Magic Mountain' Amusement Park (▶ 111) cleverly balances traditional rides with high-tech attractions on several levels of the mountaintop, and is always a fun day out for the family. Tibidabo is just one of the mountains of the Collserola range, a wonderful 6,550ha nature reserve with extensive woodlands full of wildlife. It is best reached by FGC train to Baixador de Vallvidrera. From here, it is a 10-minute walk uphill to the information centre, where details of clearly marked itineraries for walkers and cyclists are available.

VILA OLÍMPICA ✪

The 1992 Olympic Games triggered a major renovation of Barcelona's maritime façade. Just behind the Port Olímpic, the rundown district of Poble Nou was developed into the Vila Olímpica – home to 15,000 competitors during the games, and now a high-tech corridor of apartment blocks, shops and offices.

🚹 47D5
🍴 Cafés, snack bars (€–€€)
🚊 FGC Avinguda Tibidabo then Tramvia Blau to Plaça Doctor Andreu followed by the Tibidabo Funicular
Ⓦ Free
↔ Museu de la Ciència (▶ 110–11)

Amusement Park
www.tibidabo.es
✉ Parc d'Atraccions del Tibidabo, Plaça Tibidabo 3–4
☎ 93 211 79 42
🕐 Call for opening times or see website
🚋 Funicular del Tibidabo
Ⓦ Expensive

Collserola Mountains Information Centre
✉ Centre d'Informacío, Parc de Collserola
☎ 93 280 35 52
🕐 Daily 9:30–3. Closed 1 & 6 Jan, 25–26 Dec
🚊 Baixador de Vallvidrera
Ⓦ Free

The 'Magic Mountain' amusement park

🚹 47D2
✉ Vila Olímpica
🍴 Plenty (€–€€€)
🚊 Ciutadella
🚌 36, 41, 71, 92

In the Know

If you only have a short time to visit Barcelona and would like to get a real flavour of the city, here are some ideas:

10
Ways to Be a Local

Dress appropriately for Spain's most stylish city.
Learn a few words of Catalan and show interest in the regional culture.
Promenade on La Rambla (➤ 23).
Take a siesta.
Join Barcelonans for a *tertulia* (discussion) in a local café .
At weekends, visit a park or stroll along the waterfront promenades.
Follow the locals' time schedule.
Show interest in 'Barça', (➤ 54, 55).
Join in the *sardana* regional dance (➤ 69).
Develop a taste for *pa amb tomàquet* (➤ 100, panel) and *allioli* (➤ 52).

Try some tapas beside Frank Gehry's Fish sculpture

10
Top Street Sculptures

Fish, by Frank Gehry ✉ Hotel Arts, Passeig Marítim, Port Olímpica (➤ 33)
Barcelona Head, a giant mosaic sculpture by Roy Lichtenstein ✉ Passeig de Colom
Drac de la Font, Gaudí's famous 'Dragon of the Fountain' ✉ Parc Güell (➤ 21)
'La Ferralla' ('Scrap Iron'), the nickname given to the sculptural highlight of the Vila Olímpica ✉ Avinguda Icària
Gambrinus, a giant fibreglass lobster (➤ 70) by Xavier Mariscal ✉ Moll de la Fusta, Passeig de Colom
Landscape Sculptures by Beverly Pepper ✉ Parc de l'Estació del Nord
Wall by Richard Serra ✉ Plaça de la Palmera

Sardana Dancers outside the former Montjuïc Funfair ✉ Avinguda de Miramar
Dona i Ocell (Woman and Bird), in Parc Joan Miró (➤ 66)
✉ C. Tarragona
Núvol i Cadira (Cloud and Chair) on the roof of Fundació Antoni Tàpies (➤ 44) ✉ C. Aragó 255

10
Top *Tapas* Dishes

Mandonguilles (meatballs)
Boquerones and anxoves (fresh and salted anchovies)
Calamarsos amb la sevtinta (small squid cooked in their ink)
Croquetes de pollastre, or **de bacallá** (croquettes with chicken or salt cod)
Empanats and **empanadillas** (pies and deep-fried pasties with tuna filling)

La Boqueria just off La Rambla (► 49)

Gambas al ajillo (prawns with garlic)

Faves a la Catalana (broad beans, onions and *botifarra* – blood sausage – cooked in white wine)

Pa amb tomàquet (white bread with tomato and olive oil)

Pescaditos (deep-fried whitebait)

Pops a la gallega (octopus with paprika and olive oil)

10
Top Markets

La Boqueria – fruit and vegetables market ⏰ Mon–Sat 8AM–8PM. Closed Sun 🚇 Liceu (► 49)

Concepció – flowers, fruit and vegetables in the Eixample ✉ C. Aragó ⏰ Mon 8–3, Tue–Sat 8–8, Sat 8–4 🚇 Girona

Craft market ✉ Avinguda Pau Casals ⏰ First Sun of month from 10AM 🚇 Hospital Clinic

Els Encants – flea market ✉ Plaça de les Glòries ⏰ Mon, Wed, Fri, Sat 9–5

Festa de Sant Ponç – annual market of honey, herbs, natural products ✉ Carrer Hospital ⏰ 11 May 🚇 Liceu

Plaça del Pi; honey, herbs, cheeses ⏰ first and third Fri, Sat and Sun of month 10AM–10PM 🚇 Liceu

Plaça Reial – coins, stamps ⏰ Sun 10–2 🚇 Liceu

Plaça Sant Josep Oriol – art ⏰ Sat 11AM–10PM, Sun 10–3 🚇 Liceu

La Rambla – afternoon and evening craft market ⏰ Weekends only 🚇 Drassanes

Ronda Sant Antoni – coins, books, postcards and video games ⏰ Sun 9–2:30 🚇 Universitat

5
Top Rides

Bus Turístic – a good way to see the main sights if time is limited (► 121).

Fat Tire Bike Tours – fun, informal city tours by bicycle ✉ C. Escudellers 48 ☎ 93 301 36 12 ⏰ Tours daily Mar to mid-Dec from Colombus Monument.

Golondrinas – cruises around the harbour and the Olympic Port (► 72).

Telefèric – cable-car ride to Castell de Montjuïc (► 18). ⏰ Summer, daily; winter, weekends.

Tramvia Blau – Barcelona's last remaining tram grinds up the hill towards Tibidabo (► 73).

5
Top Views

Casa Milà rooftop terrace (► 37)
Columbus Monument (► 50)
Parc Güell (► 21)
Sagrada Família (► 24–25)
Torre de Collserola ☎ 93 406 93 54 ⏰ Wed–Sun 11–6

Passeig Colom from the Monument

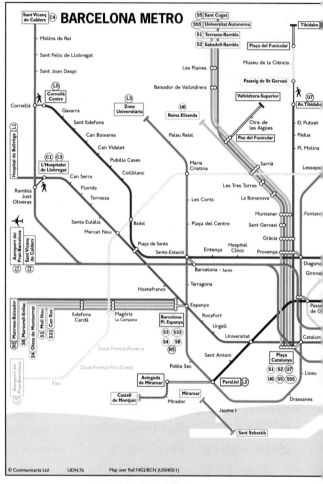

BARCELONA METRO

Barcelona's Metro

Barcelona has an impressive and efficient underground rail system, enabling you to visit most places of interest either by metro or by FGC train (► 121). Useful stations include Catalunya (for La Rambla), Barceloneta and Drassanes (for the waterfront), Jaume I (for the old city, the cathedral and Museu Picasso), Ciutadella (for the Olympic port and village), and Passeig de Gràcia (for L'Eixample).

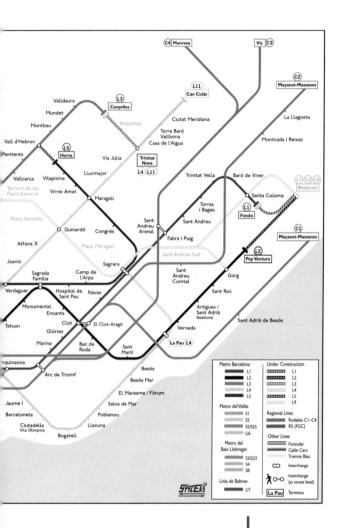

If you intend to use public transport frequently, buy one of several travelcards from any metro station or at any branch of La Caixa. The metro runs Mon–Thu, Sun and holidays 5AM–11PM; Fri, Sat and the evening before holidays 5AM–2AM. The FGC operates Mon–Thu 5:50AM–11PM; Fri–Sun 5:55AM–12:39AM. Some metro stations do not have escalators and may involve lengthy walks.

Exploring Catalonia

It would be a shame to visit Barcelona without also seeing something of Catalunya (Catalonia). Despite being an autonomous province of Spain, this unique region feels in many ways like a separate country, with its own language and deeply rooted traditions, culture and cuisine. Its geographical location makes it the gateway to Spain. Over the centuries the passage of many peoples and civilisations has shaped the region, leaving magical cities such as Girona and Tarragona brimming with historical monuments, while its beautiful landscapes have provided inspiration for such artists as Gaudí, Miró, Dalí and Picasso.

The Catalan landscape is easy to tour, and offers a wide variety of scenery, from the dramatic, snow-capped peaks of the Pyrenees and the secret bays and bustling fishing ports of the Costa Brava, north of Barcelona, to the acclaimed Penedès vineyards and long golden beaches of the Costa Daurada to the south.

'...the king, who had the sun for his hat (for it always shines in some part of his dominion), has nothing to boast of equal to Catalonia.'

PHILIP THIELENESSE,
A Year's Journey through France and Spain, 1789.

The magnificent Catedral – pride of Tarragona

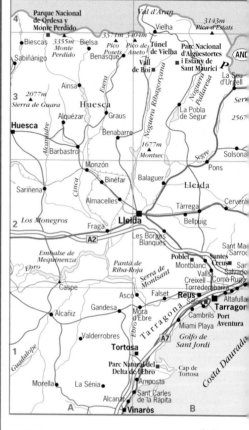

81D3

Plaça del Sol ☎ 972 50 31 55

Plenty (€–€€)

Girona (➤ 82)

Teatre-Museu Dalí

Plaça Gala-Salvador Dalí 5

972 67 75 00

Oct–Jun Tue–Sat 10:30–5:45; Jul–Sep daily 9–7:45. Closed 1 Jan and 25 Dec

None

Very expensive

FIGUERES ●●

The main claim to fame of Figueres, two hours' drive northwest of Barcelona and just 17km from the Franco-Spanish border, is that the great Surrealist painter Salvador Dalí was born here in 1904 and gave his first exhibition in the town when he was just 14. In 1974, he inaugurated his remarkable **Teatre-Museu Dalí**, located in the old municipal theatre, and to this day it remains the most visited museum in Spain after the Prado in Madrid. It is the only museum in Europe that is dedicated exclusively to his works.

The building, topped with a massive metallic dome and decorated with egg shapes, is original and spectacular – in keeping with Dalí's powerful personality. Its galleries are housed in a number of enclosed, circular tiers around a

CATALUNYA

Golfo de Léon

F

igcerda
Camprodón
Castellfollit
de la Roca
Bésalu
Ripoll   Olot   Girona
A7
l Cadí
Berga
Manlleu   Ter
Vic
Parc Natural
del Montseny
1712m
ardona   Barcelona
Caldes de
Montbui
lanresa
Granollers
errassa   Sant Pol de Mar
ualada   Arenys de Mar
Montserrat   Sabadell   Mataró
Sant Sadurní   Badalona
d'Anoia
Vilafranca   BARCELONA
del Penedès   L'Hospitalet de Llobregat
Castelldefels
Sitges
Vilanova
i la Geltrú

Portbou
San Pere de Rodes
Perelada   Cap de Creus
Roses   Cadaqués
Figueres
Golfo de Rosas
Empúries-Ampurias
L'Escala
L'Estartit
Banyoles
Peratallada
Girona   Begur
Palafrugell
Palamós
Tossa de Mar   Sant Feliu
de Guixols
Lloret de Mar
Blanes
Costa Brava

0   20   40   60 km

C   D

central stage and a courtyard containing a 'Rainy Taxi' and a tower of car tyres crowned by a boat and an umbrella. The galleries contain paintings, sculptures, jewellery, drawings and other works from his private collection along with weird and wonderful constructions from different periods of his career, including a bed with fish tails, skeletal figures and even a complete life-sized orchestra. Dalí died in Figueres in 1989, leaving his entire estate to the Spanish State. His body lies behind a simple granite slab inside the museum.

Other sights in Figueres include over 3,000 exhibits in the famous **Museu de Juguets** (Toy Museum), set inside the old Hotel Paris, and the **Museu de l'Empordà** (Art and History), which provides an informative overview of the region's art and history.

Museu de Juguets
✉ La Rambla
☎ 972 50 45 85
🕐 Tue–Sat 10–1, 4–7, Sun
and hols 11–1:30. Closed
Mon
💰 Moderate

Museu de l'Empordà
✉ La Rambla 2
☎ 972 50 23 05
🕐 Tue–Sat 11–7, Sun 11–2.
Closed Mon
💰 Cheap

Salvador Dalí
www.salvador-dali.org
An excellent website for additional tips on where to go on the surrealist route:

81

⊞ 81D3
ℹ Rambla de la Llibertat 1
☎ 972 22 65 75
🍴 Plenty (€–€€)

Catedral
✉ Plaça de la Catedral
☎ 972 21 44 26
🕐 Tue–Sat 10–2, 4–7, Sun 10–2
♿ Good 🎫 Free

Museu Arqueològic
✉ Esglesia Sant Pere de Galligans
☎ 972 20 26 32
🕐 Jun–Sep Tue–Fri 10:30–1:30, 4–7, Sat–Sun 10–2; Oct–May: Tue–Fri 10–2, 4–6, Sat–Sun 10–4
🎫 Cheap

Banys Arabs
✉ Carrer Ferran Catolic
☎ 972 21 32 62
🕐 Summer Mon–Sat 10–7, Sun 10–2; winter Mon–Sat 10–2
🎫 Cheap

Above: *Girona is a little-known gem of Catalonia*

GIRONA ●●●

Just 1½ hours by car or train from Barcelona, the beautiful, walled city of Girona is one of Catalonia's most characterful cities, with an admirable collection of ancient monuments. The old city, built on a steep hill and known for its lovely stairways, arcaded streets and sunless alleys, is separated from modern Girona by the River Onyar. The medieval, multicoloured houses overhanging the river are a photographer's dream, especially when seen from the iron footbridge designed by Eiffel. Most of the main sights are in the old city. Make sure you also allow time to shop along the beautiful Rambla de la Llibertat and to enjoy a drink in the arcaded Plaça de la Independencia.

At the heart of the old city, centred around Carrer de la Força, El Call, the old Jewish quarter, is one of the best preserved in Western Europe and is particularly atmospheric by night, with its street lanterns and intimate restaurants. Another splendid sight is the **Catedral**, with its impressive staircase leading up to a fine Baroque façade, a magnificent medieval interior and the widest Gothic vault in Europe. Housed inside another church, the **Museu Arqueològic** (Archaeological Musuem) outlines the city's history, and provides access to the Passeig Arqueològic, a panoramic walk around the walls of the old city. Near by, the 13th-century **Banys Arabs** (Arab Bathhouse), probably designed by Moorish craftsmen following the Moors' occupation of Girona, is the best preserved of its kind in Spain after the Alhambra, particularly striking for its fusion of Arab and Romanesque styles.

MONTSERRAT ✪

Fifty-six kilometres northwest of Barcelona, at the summit of Catalonia's 1,200m-high holy mountain, Montserrat – named after its strangely serrated rock formations (*mont*, mountain; *serrat*, sawed – is one of the most important pilgrimage sites in the whole of Spain. Thousands travel here every year to venerate a medieval statue of the Madonna and Child called *La Moreneta* (The Black Virgin), blackened by the smoke of millions of candles over the centuries. The statue is said to have been made by St Luke and brought to the area by St Peter, and is displayed above the altar of the monastery church.

The spectacularly sited monastery, founded in 1025, is also famous for its choir, *La Escolania*, one of the oldest and best-known boys' choirs in Europe, dating from the 13th century. The choir sings daily at 1PM in the **Basilica**, a striking edifice containing important paintings including works by El Greco and Caravaggio.

Montserrat is clearly signposted by road from Barcelona, although the most enjoyable way to get there is by FGC train from Plaça d'Espanya, followed by a thrilling cable-car ride up to the monastery.

➕ 81C2
ℹ️ Plaça de la Creu, Montserrat
☎ 93 877 77 77
🍴 Limited choice of bars and restaurants

Basilica
✉️ Monestir de Montserrat
🕐 Daily 7:30AM–7:30PM subject to change
Free
↔️ Museu de Montserrat
🕐 Mar–Dec 10–6; Jan–Feb 10–4:45
Moderate

One of Spain's principal pilgrimage destinations – within easy reach of Barcelona

Alt Penedès

Distance
105km

Time
3–3½ hours (without stops)

Start point
Vilafranca del Penedès
81C2

End point
Sant Sadurní d'Anoia
81C2

Lunch break
Sant Jordi/Ca La Katy (€€)
8½ km outside Vilafranca
del Penedès
93 899 13 26

Vilafranca del Penedès
81C2
Carrer Cort 14
93 818 12 54
Plenty (€–€€)

Sant Martí Sarroca
81B2
Plaça de l'Ajuntament 1
93 891 31 88
Limited choice (€€)

The main attraction of this drive is its magnificent scenery. Leave Vilafranca del Penedès on the BP2121 past Mas Tinell, Romagosa Torné and Torres wineries (➤ 85), until you reach Sant Martí Sarroca after 9km.

This agricultural village contains an important Romanesque church with a splendid Gothic altarpiece, and a 9th-century castle.

Continue on to Torrelles de Foix, with its tiled church dome. The road then climbs through barren scrub up to Pontons. Continue up past the Romanesque church of Valldossera, through Els Ranxox, over the Coll de la Torreta, to Santes Creus.

Santes Creus, founded in 1158 alongside the Gaia river, is one of three exceptional former Cistercian monasteries in the region (the others are Poblet and Vallbona de les Monges). Following its deconsecration, it grew into a small village in 1843 when a group of families moved into the abandoned buildings and monks' residences.

Turn right at the main road (TP2002) to El Pont d'Armentera. Join the T213 to Igualada. After 22km of breathtaking mountain scenery, turn right to La Llacuna, then left through farmland to Mediona. Continue to St Pere Sacarrera then turn right at the main road to St Quintí de Mediona. Several kilometres later, turn left to Sant Pere de Riudebitlles.

Mediona is noted for its medieval church and ruined castle, while St Pere de Riudebitlles boasts a splendid Gothic manor house – the Palace of the Marquis of Lo.

The same road eventually leads to Sant Sadurní (➤ 85).

The monastery of Santes Creus nestles among vineyards

PENEDÈS WINERIES – VILAFRANCA AND SANT SADURNÍ D'ANOIA ★

The Alt Penedès is one of Spain's most respected wine-producing areas, producing Catalonia's best-known wines and all of its *cava* (sparkling wine). Since ancient times, viticulture has been the main economic activity of its two main towns, Sant Sadurní d'Anoia and Vilafranca del Penedès.

Only half an hour's drive from Barcelona, Sant Sadurní is the centre of Catalonia's *cava* industry, with 66 *cava* firms dotted throughout the town. The largest, Codorníu, produces around 40 million bottles a year and its magnificent *Modernista* plant is open to visitors daily. Tours last 1½ hours and include a tasting.

Near by, Vilafranca del Penedès, the region's capital town, has more character than Sant Sadurní, with its fine arcaded streets and medieval mansions. In the Gothic quarter, surrounded by squares, palaces and churches, the **Museu del Vi** is the only museum in Catalonia to be wholly dedicated to

wine. Current methods of production can be observed at Vilafranca's three top wineries – **Mas Tinell, Romagosa Torné** and **Miguel Torres** – all located just outside the town centre on the BP2121 to Sant Martí Sarroca.

Museu del Vi
- Plaça Jaume I, 1 and 3, Vilafranca del Penedès
- 93 890 05 82
- Jun–Aug Tue–Sat 10–9, Sun 10–2; Sep–May Tue–Sat 10–2, 4–7, Sun 10–2
- Cheap

Penedès Wineries
- Codorníu: 93 818 32 32; Caves Romagosa Torné: 93 899 13 53; Mas Tinell: 93 817 05 86; Miguel Torres: 93 817 74 00
- Opening times vary. Phone individual wineries for details

Did you know?
Penedès produces good red (negra or tinto), white (blanc) and rosé (rosat) wines. Of the many labels, René Barbier and Miguel Torres (the region's largest, most famous producer) are reliable, and dry Bach whites are also popular. Catalan cava is labelled according to quality and sweetness – Brut Nature, Brut, Sec, and Semi-Sec which, despite its name, is very sweet and the cheapest.

Above: the Museu del Vi in Vilafranca

81C2

Carrer Sinia Morera 1

☎ 93 93 894 50 04/93 894 42 51

Plenty (€–€€)

Costa Daurada (➤ 87); Tarragona (➤ 88–90)

Museums

Cau Ferrat and Maricel de Mar: Carrer Fonolar; Romàntic: Casa Llopis, Carrer Sant Gaudenci 1

Cau Ferrat: 93 894 03 64; Romàntic: 93 894 29 69

Mid-Sep to mid-Jun Tue–Fri 10–1:30, 3–6:30, Sat 10–7, Sun 10–3; mid-Jun to mid-Sep Tue–Sun 10–2, 5–9

Few

Cau Ferrat: moderate. Maricel de Mar and Romàntic: cheap. Combined ticket available for all three museums

Romàntic: guided tours every hour

Museu Maricel de Mar houses an eclectic collection of Catalan treasures

SITGES ⭐⭐

Sitges, 40km south of Barcelona, is one of Spain's oldest bathing resorts and has long been the weekend and holiday playground of Barcelonans. It was once a sleepy fishing port and, although it has now developed into a thriving seaside destination, the old town still retains its ancient charm, with narrow streets, whitewashed cottages and flower-festooned balconies. It also boasts several appealing *Modernista* buildings.

It was artist and writer Santiago Rusinyol who first put Sitges on the map, bringing it to the attention of artists such as Manuel de Falla, Ramon Casas, Nonell, Utrillo and Picasso. Rusinyol's house, **Cau Ferrat**, is today a museum, containing works by El Greco and Picasso amongst others. Neighbouring **Museu Maricel de Mar** houses an interesting collection of medieval and baroque artefacts, including Catalan ceramics, and the nearby **Museu Romàntic** provides a fascinating insight into 18th-century patrician life in Sitges.

Sitges is famous for its beautiful Platja d'Or (Golden Beach), which stretches southwards for 5km from the baroque church of Sant Bartomeu i Santa Tecla. Its palm-fringed promenade is dotted with beach bars, cafés, and some of the coast's finest fish restaurants. However, the resort is perhaps best-known for its vibrant nightlife, drawing a young cosmopolitan crowd throughout the summer season. It is also a popular gay holiday destination. From October to May, Sitges is considerably quieter, except during *Carnaval* in mid-February when the town once more comes alive with wild parties and showy parades, drawing spectators from afar.

The Costa Daurada

The Costa Daurada (Golden Coast) takes its name from its long sandy beaches. This short drive starts in Tarragona and covers its northernmost stretch.

Leave Tarragona on the N340 coast road towards Barcelona. A few kilometres later you will arrive at the resorts of Altafulla and Torredembarra.

These two thriving holiday resorts attained great prosperity in the 18th century as a result of the wine trade with the American colonies. Note the Renaissance-style castle at Torredembarra.

Continue on the N340 for 6km. Turn left to Creixell.

The hilltop village of Creixell boasts a ruined medieval castle and a church with a striking *Modernista* belltower.

Return to the N340. After 2km, the road skirts the 2nd-century Roman Arc de Bara then continues to Coma-Ruga and Sant Salvador.

Coma-Ruga was once an area of marshland with mineral-water springs. At the turn of the 19th century two spas were established around which this bustling resort developed. The local speciality, *xató* – a scrumptious cold fish salad, with a dressing similar to *romesco* (➤ 53) – must be sampled. At Sant Salvador, the cellist Pau Casals had his summer residence; today it is a museum.

From the Museu Pau Casals, the coast road leads to Calafell, where fishing boats are launched straight from the sand. Join the N246 here (direction Barcelona) and follow signs to Vilanova i la Geltrú.

The busy commercial centre of Vilanova is also a popular resort, thanks to its sandy beach, its palm-lined seafront, and its many appealing restaurants.

Continue on the N246 to Sitges (➤ 86).

Distance
63km

Time
1 hour (without stops)

Start point
Tarragona
✚ 80B1

End point
Sitges
✚ 81C2

Lunch break
🍴 Casa Victor (€€)
✉ Passeig Marítim 23, Coma-Ruga
☎ 977 68 14 73

Long sandy beaches characterise the Costa Daurada

80B1
Plenty (€–€€)
Carrer de Fortuny 4
☎ 977 23 34 15

Tarragona

This agreeable city is surprisingly undiscovered by most foreign visitors to the region, even though it contains the largest ensemble of Roman remains in Spain, the remarkable architectural legacy of Roman Tarraco, capital of an area that once covered half the Iberian peninsula. Originally settled by Iberians and then Carthaginians, it later became the base for the Roman conquest of Spain and the main commercial centre on this stretch of the coast until Barcelona and Valencia overshadowed it, after the Christian reconquest of Spain in the early 12th century.

The town is sited on a rocky hill, sloping down to the sea. The ancient upper town contains most of the Roman ruins, some interesting museums and an attractive medieval quarter with a grand cathedral. Below the Old Town lies the modern shopping district, centred on the Rambla Nova with its smart boutiques and restaurants, and a daily fruit and vegetable market in Plaça Corsini. Below the main town, the chief attraction of the lower part of the city is the maritime district of El Serrallo with its colourful fishing fleet, traditional *Lonja* (fish auction), and dockside restaurants that serve fish fresh from the nets. The rocky coastline beyond conceals a couple of beaches, notably Platja Arrabassada and Platja Llarga.

Catalan flags hanging in a Tarragona street

What to See in Tarragona

Carrer Oleguer
☎ 977 24 25 79
🕐 Tue–Sat Apr–Jun
10–1:30, 3:30–6:30;
Jul–Sep 9–9; Oct–Mar
10:30–1:30, 3:30–5:30.
Closed Mon. Sun
Summer 9–3; Winter
10–2
♿ None
Moderate (combined
ticket)

AMFITEATRE ROMA   ✪✪

Built into the hillside overlooking the Mediterranean, the Amfiteatre Roma (Roman Amphitheatre) was where the Romans held their public spectacles, including combats between gladiators and wild animals before an audience of some 12,000 people. During the 12th century the Romanesque church of Santa Maria del Miracle was built on the site, giving the beach below its name – El Miracle. You can visit the Amfiteatre, Passeig Arqueològic, Museu d'Història, Circ Romà (▶ 90) and Casa Museu de Castellarnau (▶ 90) on a combined ticket.

Pause a while in the cool cathedral to admire its many treasures

CATEDRAL ✪

Tarragona's grandiose Catedral – a magnificent Romanesque-Gothic building, in the form of a cross – was built as the centrepiece of the *ciutat antigua* (old city).

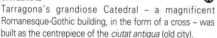

🕂 80B1
✉ Plaça de la Seu
☎ 977 23 86 85
🕐 Mon–Sat 10–1, 4–7; winter 10–2

MUSEU ARQUEOLÒGIC AND MUSEU D'HISTÒRIA ✪✪

The fascinating Museu Arqueològic (Archeological Museum) includes a section of the old Roman wall, statues of emperors, several sarcophagi and some interesting mosaics. Near by stands the Praetorium and the vaults of the 1st-century Roman Circus. The Praetorium is the site of the Museu d'Història (Tarragona History Museum), which traces the origins and history of the city through such treasures as the sarcophagus of Hipolitus, a masterpiece that was rescued from the sea in 1948.

🕂 80B1
✉ Plaça del Rei
☎ 977 23 62 09
🕐 Museu Arqueològic: Tue–Sat 10–1, 4:30–7 (8 in summer), Sun 11–2. Museu d'Història: Tue–Sat 10–5:30, Sun 10–3
♿ Moderate (combined ticket)

MUSEU I NECROPOLIA PALEOCRISTIANS ✪✪

Tarragona's most treasured Roman remains are housed in the Museu i Necropolia Paleocristians (Paleo-Christian Museum), in what was once an ancient necropolis, a 20-minute walk west of the city centre. It includes a valuable collection of mosaics, pottery, metalwork, glass and ivory.

🕂 80B1
✉ Passeig de la Independència s/n
☎ 977 21 11 75
🕐 Seasonal variations. Call for times
♿ Moderate

PASSEIG ARQUEOLÒGIC ✪✪

For an overview of the old city and the flat hinterland of the Camp de Tarragona, walk the Passeig Arqueològic, a promenade which encircles the northernmost half of the old town, around the Roman walls, of which 1km of the original 4km remains. Seven defence towers and gates still stand, giving access to the city.

🕂 80B1
✉ Passeig Arqueològic
☎ 977 24 57 96
🕐 As Amfiteatre Roma
♿ Moderate

Around Tarragona's Old Town

Distance
1½ km

Time
1 hour (without visits)

Start/end point
Ajuntament, Plaça de la Font
✚ 80B1

Coffee-break
🍴 Can Peret (€)
✉ Plaça de la Font 6
☎ 977 23 76 25

An ancient well in fascinating Tarragona

Start in Plaça de la Font. Take Carrer del Cós del Bou, at the opposite end to the Ajuntament building, up to the Circ Romà.

These ruins are all that remain of Tarragona's Roman Circus, which once occupied the Plaça de la Font.

Continue up Baixada de la Peixateria, turn right into Carrer de l'Enrajolat and immediately left into Plaça del Rei.

The Museu Arqueològic and the Museu d'Història (➤ 89) provide a useful overview of the early history of Tarragona.

A small unmarked street beside the Museu Arqueològic leads to Plaça dels Angels. From here go left, then first right along Carrer Santa Anna as far as Plaça del Forum.

Of particular interest here is a section of wall and the ruins of the Roman Forum, currently under excavation.

Take Carrer Merceria past the Gothic arches, then climb the steps to the Catedral (➤ 89). Circle this magnificent building anticlockwise. In Plaça de Palau, steps lead down to Carrer Claustre and the entrance to the Cathedral and the cloister.

The medieval cloisters here, bathed in light filtered through arches and trees, provide an atmospheric retreat from the city.

Return to Plaça de Palau. Turn left down Carrer de la Guitarra, through Plaça Sant Joan, along Baixada del Roser (alongside the old city wall) and left into Plaça del Paillol. Follow the road round into Carrer dels Cavalers past Casa Castellarnau (one of Tarragona's finest medieval mansions). A right turn into Carrer Major swings round into Baixada Misericordia and brings you back to the main square, Plaça de la Font.

Where To...

Above: *La Rambla by night*
Right: *Gaudí wall plaque at the entrance to Parc Güell*

Barcelona

Prices

Restaurant prices are approximate, based on a three-course meal for one without drinks and service. All the cafés and *tapas* bars fall under the (€) category unless marked to the contrary.

€   = €12
€€ = €12–24
€€€ = over €24

Most restaurants offer a fixed price meal (*menú del día*) of around €6 – usually including a choice of appetiser, main course, dessert and wine – which is great value but restrictive. Eating *à la carte* is more expensive but it enables you to try some of the unusual dishes. Usually the price on the menu includes VAT (IVA). If not, it should be clearly displayed on the menu. After the meal, leave a tip of about 10 per cent of the total bill, depending on quality and service.

Restaurants

Old City

Abac (€€€)
The elegance, spaciousness and minimalism of Abac's stylish cream-and-orange dining room provides a perfect backdrop for the fine Spanish haute cuisine of local chef Xavier Pellicier.
✉ Carrer Rec 79–89 ☎ 93 319 66 00 🕐 Closed Sun, Aug and Mon mid-Sep
Ⓜ Barceloneta

Agut d'Avignon (€€€)
Hidden up an alleyway off Calle d'Avinyó at the heart of the Barri Gòtic, with classic Catalan cuisine that attracts politicians, artists, and even the King of Spain.
✉ Carrer Trinitat 3 ☎ 93 302 60 34 Ⓜ Jaume I

Amaya (€€€)
Popular Basque restaurant, featuring *angulas* (baby eels) and *besugo* (sea bream). Wash it down with one of the many regional wines.
✉ La Rambla 20–24 ☎ 93 302 10 37 Ⓜ Liceu

Bio-Center (€)
The best-known of Barcelona's very few vegetarian restaurants, the Bio-Center serves a range of delicious soups, casseroles and salads.
✉ Carrer Pintor Fortuny 25 ☎ 93 301 45 83 🕐 Mon–Sat 1–5 Ⓜ Catalunya

Brasserie Flo (€€)
Famous French-founded brasserie. House specialities include *foie gras* and Alsatian-style ham with *choucroute* (sauerkraut).
✉ Carrer Jonqueres 10 ☎ 93 319 31 02 Ⓜ Urquinaona

Café de l'Academia (€€)
One of Barcelona's best-value restaurants, with generous helpings of delicious Mediterranean cuisine in the heart of the old city.
✉ Carrer Lledó 1 ☎ 93 315 00 26 🕐 Closed weekends and 2 weeks Aug Ⓜ Jaume I

Can Culleretes (€€)
One of the oldest restaurants in the city (1786), traditionally decorated with wrought-iron chandeliers and signed photographs of visiting celebrities. Among the highlights of the Catalan cuisine on the menu is *perdiz* (partridge).
✉ Carrer Quintana 5 ☎ 93 317 30 22 🕐 Lunch: Tue–Sun 1:30–4; dinner: Tue–Sat 9–11PM. Closed 3 weeks Jul Ⓜ Liceu

Ca l'Isidre (€€€)
Sophisticated bistro offering exceptional Catalan cuisine and an extensive wine list.
✉ Carrer Les Flors 120 ☎ 93 441 11 39 🕐 Closed Sun and hols Ⓜ Paral.lel (best by taxi)

Los Caracoles (€€)
Popular with both tourists and locals, and particularly famous for its robust, country-style cuisine, especially the spit-roasted chicken, and its namesake, snails.
✉ Carrer Escudellers 14 ☎ 93 302 31 85 Ⓜ Drassanes, Liceu

Casa Leopoldo (€€€)
Family-run seafood restaurant, in seedy location in the Barri Xinés. Arrive by taxi! Its *tapas* bar is also hugely popular, with its barnacles, cuttlefish and baby eels.
✉ Carrer Sant Rafael 24

☎ 93 441 30 14 🕐 Tue–Sat 1:30–4, 9–11; Sun 1:30–4 Ⓜ Liceu

La Cuineta (€€)
Well-established restaurant in the Barri Gòtic, serving authentic dishes from northeastern Spain.Good-value fixed-price menu.
✉ Carrer Pietat 12 ☎ 93 315 01 11 Ⓜ Jaume 1

Egipte (€€)
This small restaurant on La Rambla serves good-value, hearty Catalan cuisine such as cod in a cream sauce, shellfish gratin or stuffed aubergine. Try to save room for the homemade ice cream.
✉ La Rambla 79 ☎ 93 317 95 45 Ⓜ Liceu

L'Eucaliptus (€)
A two-storey, traditional tiled brasserie, offering a simple menu of torradas (toasted open sandwiches) and escalivada (traditional pepper and aubergine dish) just off La Rambla.
✉ Carrer Bonsuccés 4 ☎ 93 302 18 24 🕐 Closed Sun eves and Mon Ⓜ Catalunya

La Fonda (€–€€)
One of Ciutat Vella's most popular restaurants, with good, yet affordable Catalan food in stylish - surroundings. Be prepared to queue.
✉ Carrer Escudellers 10 ☎ 93 301 75 15 Ⓜ Liceu

La Gardunya (€)
Impressive seafood platters and an excellent-value menú del día makes this the Boqueria market's most celebrated restaurant.
✉ Carrer Jerusalem 18 ☎ 93 302 43 23 🕐 Closed Sun Ⓜ Liceu

Govinda (€)
An Indian vegetarian restaurant near La Rambla.

✉ Plaça Vila de Madrid 4–5 ☎ 93 318 77 29 🕐 Lunch: daily 1–4; dinner: Tue–Sat 8:30–11:45 Ⓜ Catalunya

El Gran Café (€€)
Classic restaurant, serving French and Catalan cuisine in grand turn-of-the-19th-century surroundings.
✉ Carrer d'Avinyó 9 ☎ 93 318 79 86 🕐 Closed Sun Ⓜ Liceu

Hofmann (€€€)
Interpretations of regional dishes by Mey Hofmann, one of Spain's most talented chefs, who also runs a world-renowned cookery school on the premises.
✉ Carrer Argenteria 74–78 ☎ 93 319 58 89 🕐 Closed Sat, Sun and Aug Ⓜ Jaume I
❓ Phone for details of special two-day cookery courses

L'Ou com Balla (€€)
Hidden down a back street of La Ribera near Santa Maria del Mar, the friendly staff at this cosy, candlelit restaurant promise a night to remember with their culinary delights, including a variety of regional dishes.
✉ Carrer Banys Vells 20 ☎ 93 310 53 78 Ⓜ Jaume I

El Paraguayo (€€)
Specialities from Paraguay and Argentina, including barbecued meat served on wooden boards for carnivores, and salads and pastas for vegetarians.
✉ Carrer Parc 1 ☎ 93 302 14 41 🕐 Closed Mon Ⓜ Drassanes

La Perla Nera (€€)
Authentic flavours, perfect pastas and an attractive dining room, brimming with fresh flowers are the trademark of this well-respected Italian restaurant.
✉ Via Laietana 32–4 ☎ 93 310 56 46 Ⓜ Jaume I

Opening Times
The restaurants on these pages are all open for lunch and dinner daily unless otherwise stated. Most establishments serve lunch from around 1 to 3:30 or 4. Dinner normally starts at 8:30 or 9, and is often served until midnight or the early hours of the morning. Many cafés and tapas bars remain open from early morning until late at night. It is advisable to book in most restaurants, especially at weekends. Nearly all restaurants close briefly for annual holidays (dates not listed) so phone first to avoid disappointment.

Where Should We Go?
In the Old City and Gràcia, you will find generally small, reasonably priced restaurants. The Eixample is more up-market, but it also has a smattering of cheaper eateries, fast-food joints and some excellent tapas bars. For seafood, try La Barceloneta for traditional atmosphere or, for something more sophisticated, the Port Olímpic.

Dinner in La Barceloneta

'There is an undeniable charm in the *chiringuitos* (seafood restaurants) lining the beach like dominoes at the sea's edge... and the crowds on seemingly perpetual vacation strolling to and fro... one goes to La Barceloneta as much for the ambience as the food.' (*Llorenç Torrado, local journalist*)

El Pintor (€€)

Serving traditional Catalan cuisine, fine regional wines, El Pintor is housed in a cosy, brick-vaulted interior with crisp white linen and candlelight.

✉ **Carrer St Honorat 7** ☎ **93 301 40 65** 🚇 **Jaume I**

Pitarra (€)

An old-fashioned Spanish restaurant in the Barri Gòtic, named after the 19th-century Catalan playwright who lived and wrote his plays and poetry here. They serve a particularly good Valencian paella.

✉ **Carrer d'Avinyó 56** ☎ **93 301 16 47** 🕐 **Closed Sun and Aug** 🚇 **Liceu**

Els Quatre Gats (€€)

Many famous artists and intellectuals used to gather in this popular *Modernista* café in the early 1900s. Even the menu was designed by Picasso.

✉ **Carrer Montsió 3 bis** ☎ **93 302 41 40** 🚇 **Catalunya**

Les Quinze Nits (€€)

Under the same management as La Fonda (► 93), this wood-panelled restaurant with an attractive terrace serves an excellent Catalan style *civet de conill* (rabbit stew) and an impressive *parillada de peix* (seafood mixed grill).

✉ **Plaça Reial 6** ☎ **93 317 30 75** 🚇 **Liceu**

Quo Vadis (€€€)

One of Barcelona's finest restaurants, near the Boqueria market, serving time-tested recipes from all over Spain.

✉ **Carrer Carme 7** ☎ **93 302 40 72** 🕐 **Closed Sun and Aug** 🚇 **Liceu**

La Rioja (€–€€)

This bright, white-tiled restaurant offers a splendid selection of Riojan dishes and wines, and a good-value *menú del día*.

✉ **Carrer Duran i Bas 5** ☎ **93 301 22 98** 🕐 **Closed Sat eve, Sun and Aug** 🚇 **Catalunya**

Sushi-Ya (€€)

Small Japanese restaurant, serving the usual *sushi*, *sashimi*, *tempura* and *miso* soup.

✉ **Carrer Quintana 4** ☎ **93 412 72 49** 🚇 **Liceu**

Taxidermista (€€)

Buzzy designer restaurant in an old taxidermist's studio, offering modern Mediterranean dishes such as lamb couscous or duck breast with truffle vinaigrette.

✉ **Plaça Reial 8** ☎ **93 412 45 36** 🕐 **Closed Mon and 3 weeks Aug** 🚇 **Liceu**

Venus (€–€€)

This bright, cheerful neighbourhood bar prides itself on its authentic cuisine from all around the Mediterranean basin, including Greece, Africa and Turkey.

✉ **Carrer Avinyó 25** ☎ **93 301 15 85** 🚇 **Jaume 1**

Seafront

Agua (€€)

Located right on the Barceloneta beach, near the Port Olímpic (► 33). The menu is creative, yet also offers excellent traditional Barceloneta fare, with the emphasis on rice-based dishes.

✉ **Passeig Marítim de la Barceloneta 30** ☎ **93 225 12 72** 🚇 **Ciutadella**

Bestial (€€)

Fabulous Italian bistro with extensive wood decking, palm trees and parasol topped tables, all with views of Frank Gehry's golden fish.

✉ **Carrer Ramon Trias Fargas 2–4** ☎ **93 224 04 07** 🚇 **Ciutadella-Vila Olímpica**

Cal Pinxo (€€€)

This former beach bar has been transformed into a fashionable seafood restaurant facing Barceloneta beach, where paella and fish dishes can be enjoyed on a large terrace in summer.

✉ **Carrer Baluard 124** ☎ **93 221 50 28** 🚇 **Barceloneta**

El Cangrejo Loco (€€)

Popular fish restaurant at the far end of the Port Olímpic but worth the walk for its extensive *pica-pica* starters and delicious main dishes – try the *fideua*, cod fried in honey.

✉ **Moll de Gregal 29–30, Port Olímpic** ☎ **93 221 05 33** 🚇 **Ciutadella**

Can Majó (€€€)

The city's top seafood restaurant, in La Barceloneta. The *suquet de peix* (mixed fish casserole), *arrozes* (black rice) with *bacalao* (salt cod) or lobster, and *centollos* (crabs from the north coast) are truly delicious.

✉ **Carrer Almirall Aixada 23** ☎ **93 221 54 55** 🕐 **Closed Sun eve and Mon** 🚇 **Barceloneta**

Emperador (€€€)

One of the best of the new harbourside restaurants in the extremely fashionable Palau de Mar (▶ 58), with outdoor tables and a variety of fish and seafood dishes.

✉ **Palau de Mar, Plaça Pau Vila 1** ☎ **93 221 02 20** 🚇 **Barceloneta**

Julius (€€€)

Up-market, Scandinavian styled bar serving first class fish and seafood tapas, and delicious rice dishes.

✉ **Passeig Joan de Borbó 66** ☎ **93 224 70 35** 🚇 **Barceloneta**

El Passadís d'el Pep (€€€)

There's no menu as such here, just some of the best fish in town. Choose from bream, bass, oysters, shellfish or the catch of the day.

✉ **Pla del Palau 2** ☎ **93 310 10 21** 🕐 **Closed Sun, hols and 3 weeks Aug** 🚇 **Barceloneta**

San Fermín (€€)

A rustic Basque restaurant by the Port Olímpic. You'll find cider poured from the barrel and huge T-bone steaks cooked on an outdoor grill.

✉ **Moll de Gregal 22** ☎ **93 221 05 43** 🚇 **Ciutadella**

Set Portes (€€€)

One of Barcelona's most historic restaurants, with waiters in long white aprons, serving excellent Catalan cuisine in traditional surroundings. It has always attracted an illustrious clientele.

✉ **Passeig de Isabel II, 14** ☎ **93 319 30 33** 🚇 **Barceloneta**

Eixample & Gràcia

Asador de Burges (€€€)

A traditional Castilian roast house where lamb and suckling pig are cooked in a brick oven until they are tender to the touch. Another speciality is *cocido castellano*, a hearty stew of meat, sausages and chickpeas.

✉ **Carrer Bruc 118** ☎ **93 207 31 60** 🕐 **Closed Sun; Mon and Tue evening** 🚇 **Verdaguer**

Beltxenea (€€€)

Barcelona's premier Basque restaurant is set in an elegant 19th-century *Modernista* building and features a pretty interior garden terrace.

✉ **Carrer Mallorca 275** ☎ **93 215 30 24** 🕐 **Closed Sat lunch, all day Sun, Aug and public hols** 🚇 **Diagonal, Passeig de Gràcia**

Tapas

The term *tapas* is thought to come from the habit of having a snack with a pre-meal drink to *tapar el apetito* ('put a lid on the appetite'). *Tapas* consist of small portions of fish, meat or vegetables, whereas *raciones* are bigger portions and usually enough for a light meal.

A Sweet Tooth

Catalan desserts are often uninspiring – a choice between *gelat* (ice cream), *flam* (crème caramel), *crèma catalana* (crème brulée), *macedonia* (fruit salad) or *formatge* (cheese). But look out for *mel i mató* (curd cheese with honey), *postre de músic* (spiced fruit cake), *panellets* (marzipans), *torrons* (nougats) and *cocas* (pastries sprinkled with sugar and pine-nuts).

Botafumeiro (€€€)

This Galician seafood restaurant serves fish (flown in daily from Galicia) with regional wines and Catalan *cavas*. The *mariscos Botafumeira* (seafood platter) is a sight to behold.

✉ Carrer de Gran de Gràcia 81 ☎ 93 218 42 30 🚇 Fontana

El Caballito Blanco (€)

The 'Little White Horse' is a cheerful, good-value, traditional restaurant, always packed with locals.

✉ Carrer Mallorca 196 ☎ 93 453 10 33 🕐 Closed Sun eve, Mon and Aug 🚇 Hospital Clinic

Casi Casi (€)

An Andalusian restaurant in Gracia. Try the excellent gazpacho or *ajoblanco* (cold garlic soup) to start, followed by the daily catch *a la Andaluza*.

✉ Carrer Laforja 8 ☎ 93 415 81 94 🚇 Gràcia

Casa Calvet (€€€€)

Gaudí's first apartment building in Barcelona is now a sumptuous, formal restaurant offering sophisticated French and Catalan cuisine.

✉ Carrer Casp 48 ☎ 93 412 40 12 🕐 Closed Sun 🚇 Urquinaona

La Dama (€€€)

The French cuisine of this Michelin star-rated restaurant rivals that of the top restaurants of Paris. An added bonus is the exceptional *Modernista* setting.

✉ Avinguda Diagonal 423 ☎ 93 202 06 86 🚇 Provença

FrescCo (€)

Eat-as-much-as-you-want from the self-service salads, pasta, pizza, ice cream, bread and beverages. Take-away service also available. Founded by Jordi Arrese,

silver medallist in the Barcelona Olympics. Also at Ronda Universitat 29.

✉ Carrer València 263 ☎ 93 488 10 49 🚇 Passeig de Gràcia

El Glop (€)

Crowded restaurant serving chargrilled meat and seasonal vegetables at reasonable prices, washed down with Catalan wines.

✉ Carrer Sant Lluís 24 (also at Carrer Casp 21 and Rambla Catalunya 65) ☎ 93 213 70 58 🕐 Closed Mon 🚇 Joanic

Jean Luc Figueras (€€€€)

Exquisite culinary delights served in striking surroundings of tangerine and pale-green ceramics, and enhanced by original art deco silverware.

✉ Carrer Santa Teresa 10 ☎ 93 415 28 77 🕐 Closed Sun, 3 weeks Aug 🚇 Diagonal

Madrid-Barcelona (€€)

Charming café-restaurant in a converted railway station. Dishes are served *a la brasa* – cooked on a coal-fired range.

✉ Carrer d'Aragó 282 ☎ 93 215 70 27 🕐 Closed Sun 🚇 Passeig de Gràcia

Mandalay-Café (€€)

Fun and funky, this restaurant fuses Thai, Vietnamese and Indonesian cuisine with Mediterranean ingredients and entertains with trapeze artists on Fridays and Saturdays.

✉ Carrer Provença 330 ☎ 93 458 60 17 🚇 Verdaguer, Diagonal

El Racó d'en Freixa (€€€)

Highly original cooking makes this one of the city's most popular Sunday-lunch haunts. Save room for the puddings which come in threes – bananas, fried, baked and caramelised, or a trio of iced, warm and hot chocolate delights.

✉ **Carrer Sant Elies 22**
☎ 93 209 75 59 🕐 Closed
Sun, Mon & Aug 🚇 Plaça
Molina/Sant Gervasi

Suburbs

Alkimia (€€€)
Barcelona's most exciting
new comer with chef Jordi
Vila at the helm, serving
wonderfully innovative
dishes in a sleek, minimal
dining room.

✉ **Carrer Industria 79** ☎ 93
207 61 15 🚇 Verdaguer,
Hospital Sant Pau, Sagrada
Familia

La Balsa (€€€)
International cuisine served
at the top of this circular
tower, originally built as a
water cistern.

✉ **Carrer Infanta Isabel 4, Sant
Gervasi** ☎ 93 211 50 48
🕐 Closed Mon lunch, Aug
lunch & Sun 🚇 Tibidabo

La Bodeguita del Poble (€€)
One of several theme
restaurants in the Poble
Espanyol (➤ 22), this one
offers Cuban market
cooking such as pork, beans
and rice.

✉ **Poble Espanyol** ☎ 93 426
38 45 🚌 13, 50, 61

Can Travinou (€€€)
Set in a beautiful 18th-century
masia (farmhouse) and
garden, on a hill above
Horta. The wine list extends
to 500 wines and *cavas*.

✉ **Carrer Jorge Manrique s/n**
☎ 93 428 03 01 🕐 Closed Sun
eve 🚇 Montbau

Gaig (€€€)
A famous family-run
restaurant, founded in
1869 as a café for cart
drivers. It is now one of
Barcelona's most up-market
eateries.

✉ **Passeig Maragall 402**
☎ 93 429 10 17 🕐 Closed
Sun eve, Mon & 3 weeks Aug
🚇 Vilapicina

Neichel (€€€)
This stylish restaurant boasts
the talents of Alsace-born
chef Jean-Louis Neichel,
who has been described as
'the most brilliant ambas-
sador French cuisine has
ever had within Spain'.

✉ **Carrer Beltrán í Rózpide 16
bis** ☎ 93 203 84 08 🕐 Closed
Sun, Mon, Aug and hols
🚇 Palau Reial

La Parra (€–€€)
Country cooking in an old
coaching inn with hearty
portions of lamb, rabbit, steak
and spare ribs cooked on a
giant wood-fired grill, and
served with lashings of
homemade *allioli* (➤ 52).

✉ **Carrer Joanot Martorell 3,
Hostafranca** ☎ 93 332 51 34
🕐 Closed Aug, Mon, Tue–Fri
lunch and Sun eve
🚇 Hostafranca

La Venta (€€€)
The conservatory and
terrace, and the light,
imaginative menu, make for
perfect spring lunches and
relaxing summer evenings.

✉ **Plaça Dr Andreu, Sant
Gervasi** ☎ 93 212 64 55
🕐 Closed Sun 🚇 Avinguda
Tibidabo then Tramvia Blau

Cafés and Tapas Bars

Old City

Ambos Mundos
Pleasant *cerveceria* (beer
bar) in Plaça Reial serving
wholesome tapas in
terracotta dishes.

✉ **Plaça Reial 9–10** ☎ 93 317
01 66 🕐 Closed Tue eve 🚇
Liceu

Bar del Pi
Simple but popular, despite
its small *tapas* selection, in
one of Barcelona's most
atmospheric squares.

✉ **Plaça Sant Josep Oriol 1**
☎ 93 302 21 23 🕐 Closed
Tue, 2 weeks Jan and 2 weeks
Aug 🚇 Liceu

'Cafè Sol, Per Favor'
Start the day with a *cafè
amb llet* (a large milky
coffee). After mid-
morning, drink a *tallat* (a
small coffee with a dash of
milk), a *cafè sol* (espresso)
or a *cafè americano*.
Descafeinado is widely
available but order it *de
máquina* (espresso-style).
After dinner, why not try a
carajillo (a *sol* with a shot
of brandy)?

Bodegas, Cervecerias and Orxaterias

There are bars on every second street in Barcelona – cosy, old-fashioned *bodegas*, serving wine from the barrel, and *cervecerias* or beer bars, offering both local beer on draught (*una cana*) and pricier imported beers. Or visit an *orxateria* and try *orxata*, the refreshing, milk-like drink made from crushed *chufa* nuts, and unique to Spain.

El Bosc de les Fades

An extraordinary café-cum-magic fairy world, decorated with fountains, toadstools and fairytale princesses.

✉ Passatge de la Banca, La Rambla 4–6 ☎ 93 317 26 49 🚇 Drassanes

Cafè de l'Òpera

This original 19th-century café is one of Barcelona's favourites, and the best terrace-café along the Ramblas.

✉ La Rambla 74 ☎ 93 302 41 80 🚇 Liceu

Café Zurich

Popular bar and meeting place at the top of La Rambla. A great place for people-watching and soaking up the atmosphere.

✉ Plaça Catalunya 1 ☎ 93 317 91 53 🚇 Catalunya

Celta

A Galician bar near the port, known for its fried *rabas* (squid) and its *patatas bravas*, (potatoes in a spicy mayonnaise), serving Galician white wine in traditional white ceramic cups.

✉ Carrer Mercè 16 ☎ 93 315 00 06 🕐 Closed Sun 🚇 Drassanes, Barceloneta

Dulcinea

The most famous chocolate shop in town. Try *melindros* (sugar-topped sponge fingers) dipped in very thick hot chocolate.

✉ Carrer Petritxol 2 ☎ 93 302 68 24 🚇 Liceu

Forn de Betlem

A bright orange, trendy café and cake shop near the Museum of Contemporary Art (► 50), one of very few places around the museum where you can stop for a coffee or a snack.

✉ Carrer Joaquín Costa 34 🚇 Universitat

Hard Rock Café

The latest addition to the world-famous chain.

✉ Plaça de Catalunya 21 ☎ 93 270 23 05 🚇 Catalunya

Hivernacle

Elegant café inside the Parc de la Ciutadella's beautiful 19th-century greenhouse. Occasional live jazz or classical music.

✉ Parc de la Ciutadella ☎ 93 295 40 17 🕐 Closed Sun eve 🚇 Arc de Triomf

Irati

One of the city's best-loved bars for sumptuous *pintxos* (Basque *tapas*) washed down with txacoli (Basque country semi-sparkling wine) and the locally brewed cider.

✉ Carrer Cardenal Casañas 17 ☎ 93 302 30 84 🚇 Liceu

Mesón del Café

Join locals at the bar for a coffee or hot chocolate while exploring the Barri Gòtic.

✉ Carrer de la Libreteria 16 ☎ 93 315 07 54 🕐 Closed Sun 🚇 Jaume I

La Plata

One of several *tascas* (traditional bars) on this narrow medieval street, specialising in whitebait, anchovies, and tomato and onion salads.

✉ Carrer Mercè 28 ☎ 93 315 10 09 🕐 Closed Sun 🚇 Barceloneta

Sagardi

A spacious new bar, popular with the young pre-dinner crowd, or for those wishing to make a meal out of their large, tasty portions of *tapas*.

✉ Carrer Argentería 62 ☎ 93 319 99 93 🕐 Closed Sat 🚇 Jaume I

Tèxtil Cafè

Delicious quiches and salads, in the courtyard of the medieval palace which houses the Museu Tèxtil.

☒ **Carrer Montcada 12** ☎ 93 268 25 98 🕐 **Closed Mon** 🚇 **Jaume I** ❓ **No need to pay museum entrance**

La Vinya del Senyor

A modern, stand-up wine bar beside Santa Maria del Mar.

☒ **Plaça Santa Maria 5** ☎ 93 310 33 79 🕐 **Closed Mon** 🚇 **Jaume I**

Seafront
Can Ramonet

This is a stand-up *tapas* bar in one of La Barceloneta's top fish restaurants. It is worth trying their mussels, 'from the beach'.

☒ **Carrer Maquinista 17**
☎ **93 319 30 64**
🚇 **Barceloneta**

Forn de Betlem

This tucked away bakery serves a range of rustic loaves from Finnish multi-grains to German rye, as well as a great range of sandwiches and snacks to takeaway. Perfect for picnics.

☒ **Carrer Xuclà 23** ☎ **93 302 27 82** 🕐 **Mon-Sat 7AM-9PM**
🚇 **Catalunya**

El Rey de la Gamba

The 'King of Prawns' serves seafood and cured hams. Busy at weekends.

☒ **Passeig Joan de Borbó 53 (also Moll Mistral, Port Olímpic)**
☎ **93 221 73 06**
🚇 **Barceloneta**

El Vaso del Oro

One of very few *cervecerias* (beer bars) that brews its own beers.

☒ **Carrer Balboa 6** ☎ **93 319 30 98** 🚇 **Barceloneta**

Eixample & Gràcia
Ba-Ba-Reeba

The *tapas* selection here includes prawns wrapped in bacon and sea urchins filled with melted cheese.

☒ **Passeig de Gràcia 28**
☎ **93 301 43 02** 🚇 **Passeig de Gràcia**

Bodega Sepúlveda

Boquerones (fresh anchovies) are the speciality at this genuine locals' bar.

☒ **Carrer Sepúlveda 173 bis**
☎ **93 323 59 44** 🕐 **Closed Sun & 3 weeks Aug** 🚇 **Universitat**

La Bodegueta

An old wine tavern, well known for its charcuterie and local wines and vermouths.

☒ **Rambla de Catalunya 100**
☎ **93 215 48 94** 🕐 **Closed Sun lunch** 🚇 **Provença**

Ciudat Condal Cerveceria

A popular meeting-place in the centre of town for breakfast or coffee.

☒ **Rambla de Catalunya 18**
☎ **93 318 19 97** 🚇 **Catalunya**

Flash-Flash Tortilleria (€)

The place for cheap, healthy Spanish fast food – *tortillas* (omelettes) and salad.

☒ **Carrer Granada del Penedes 25** ☎ **93 237 09 90**
🚇 **Diagonal**

Pla de la Garsa

A former 16th-century stables and dairy near the Picasso Museum (▶ 20) now a beautiful bar-restaurant, known for its cheeses, pâtés and hams.

☒ **Carrer Assaonadors 13**
☎ **93 315 24 13** 🕐 **Closed lunch** 🚇 **Jaume I**

Qu-Qu (Quasi Queviures)

A delicatessen-cum-*tapas* bar, specialising in salads, cheeses and Catalan sausage meats.

☒ **Passeig de Gràcia 24**
☎ **93 317 45 12** 🚇 **Passeig de Gràcia**

Tapa Tapa

The place to meet for *tapas* and a beer. Specials include snails, fried pig snout, black squid and octopus.

☒ **Passeig de Gràcia 44**
☎ **93 488 33 69** 🚇 **Passeig de Gràcia**

Regional Cuisine

Barcelona boasts restaurants to suit all tastes, budgets and occasions. Contrary to what many visitors assume, there is no such thing as 'Spanish national cuisine' but rather a wide variety of regional styles, such as Galician, Basque, Castilian and Andalucian, all to be found in Barcelona.

Catalonia

Pa amb Tomàquet
No Catalan meal is complete without *pa amb tomàquet* – a hearty slice (*llesque*) of white country bread rubbed with a ripe tomato, with a drizzle of olive oil and a pinch of salt. There are even restaurants called *llesqueria*, which specialise solely in '*pa-amb-t*' with a variety of toppings.

Restaurants and Cafés/Bars

Girona
L'Arcada (€)
Chic café bar-cum-restaurant underneath Rambla Llibertat's handsome arcade.
✉ Rambla Llibertat 38 ☎ 972 20 10 15

Cipresaia (€€)
Smart, sophisticated restaurant, at the heart of the old Jewish quarter.
✉ Carrer General Fornas 2 ☎ 972 22 24 49 🕔 Closed Thu

El Pou de Call (€€)
Local cuisine in traditional surroundings. Excellent-value *menú del diá* and wine list.
✉ Carrer de la Força 14 ☎ 972 22 37 74 🕔 Closed Sun eve

Montserrat
Abat Cisneros (€€)
Montserrat's top restaurant. The 16th-century stone dining-room used to contain the monastery stables.
✉ Hotel Abat Cisneros ☎ 93 877 77 01

Sitges
Chiringuito (€)
A traditional-style *tapas* bar in a wooden hut on the seafront, specialising in fresh sardines and salads
✉ Passeig de la Ribera ☎ 93 894 75 96

Mare Nostrum (€€)
Smart waterfront restaurant. Try the *Xato de Sitges* (grilled fish with a local variant of *romesco* sauce, ▶ 53), or monkfish and prawns with garlic mousseline.
✉ Passeig de la Ribera 60–62 ☎ 93 894 33 93 🕔 Closed Wed & mid-Dec to end Jan

Tarragona
Bodega Celler Gras (€)
A good place to join the locals for *tapas* specialities – pâtés, cheeses and *charcuterie*, including spicy *xoriço* and Mallorquin *sobrassada*.
✉ Carrer Governadir Gonzalez 8 ☎ 977 23 48 20 🕔 Closed Sun eve

Bufet el Tiberi (€–€€)
Kitsch but fun, this Catalan theme restaurant comes complete with staff in traditional dress. The food is unexceptional but is a good bet for travellers on a budget.
Carrer Martí d'Ardenya 5 ☎ 977 23 54 03 🕔 Closed Sun eve, Mon

Estació Marítima (€€€)
This is one of the best of the many fish restaurants and tapas bars that line the waterfront in the fishermen's district of Serralló.
✉ Moll de Costa Tinglade 4 ☎ 977 22 74 18 🕔 Closed Sun eve and Mon

Sol-Ric (€€)
Excellent fish restaurant located on the outskirts of town near Platja Rembassada.
✉ Via Augusta 227 ☎ 977 23 20 32 🕔 Closed Mon eve, Sun

Vilafranca del Penedès
Cal Ton (€€)
It may come as a surprise to find such a smart, modern restaurant in an otherwise traditional town. Try the mouth-watering pancakes filled with a seafood and *cava* sauce.
✉ Carrer del Casal 8 ☎ 93 890 37 41 🕔 Closed Sun eve and Mon, Easter week, 2 Aug

Barcelona

Arts Barcelona (€€€)
Barcelona's most fashionable hotel provides state-of-the-art, unabashed luxury beside the sea (▶ panel).
www.ritzcarlton.com
✉ Carrer de la Marina 19–21
☎ 93 221 10 00
🚇 Ciutadella/Vila Olímpica

Barcelona Hilton (€€€)
High-amenity hotel, 15 minutes from the airport, at the heart of the city's commercial and financial district.
www.hilton.com
✉ Avinguda Diagonal 589–591
☎ 93 495 77 77 🚇 Maria Cristina

Citadines (€€)
A 3-star 'aparthotel' on the Ramblas, with a rooftop terrace overlooking part of the Old City (▶ 102).
www.citadines.com
✉ La Rambla 122 ☎ 93 270 11 11 🚇 Catalunya/Liceu

Claris (€€€)
Just off the exclusive Passeig de Gràcia, this impressive hotel features modern accommodation furnished in marble, glass and works of art. Several restaurants, a roof terrace with pool, a fitness centre, a Japanese garden and even a museum of priceless Egyptian antiques.
www.derbyhotels.es
✉ Carrer Pau Clarís 150
☎ 93 487 62 62
🚇 Passeig de Gràcia

Colón (€€–€€€)
Old-fashioned, family-friendly hotel, opposite the cathedral. Country-home feel rather than that of a busy city hotel.
www.hotelcolon.es
✉ Avenida de la Catedral 7
☎ 93 301 14 04 🚇 Jaume I/ Urquinaona

Condes De Barcelona (€€€)
Stylish hotel in Barcelona's main shopping district. Elegant public rooms, and bedrooms furnished in *Modernista* style.
www.condesdebarcelona.es
✉ Passeig de Gràcia 73–75
☎ 93 467 47 80 🚇 Diagonal

Duques De Bergara (€€)
Contemporary elegance in a turn-of-the-19th-century building. Four stars.
www.hoteles-catalonia.es
✉ Carrer Bergara 11 ☎ 93 301 51 51 🚇 Catalunya

Gallery (€€€)
You'll get a warm welcome and relaxing stay at this lovely hotel. Ask for their leaflet with five city strolls.
www.galleryhotel.com
✉ Carrer Rosselló 249
☎ 93 415 99 11
🚇 Diagonal

Gaudí (€€)
Facing Palau Güell, one of Gaudí's masterworks, this modern 3-star hotel has 73 well-equipped rooms and a Gaudí-inspired reception area.
www.hotelgaudi.es
✉ Carrer Nou de la Rambla 12
☎ 93 317 90 32
🚇 Drassanes/Liceu

Gran Hotel Barcino (€€€)
Modern luxury and tasteful rooms await you here in the heart of the Barri Gòtic.
www.gargallo-hotels.com
✉ Carrer Jaume I, 6 ☎ 93 302 20 12; 🚇 Jaume I

Gran Vía (€)
It is easy to imagine how splendid this reasonably priced hotel must have been in its heyday, with its old-world gilt, balustraded staircase and chandeliers.

Prices
Prices are based on the cost of a double room per night (excluding breakfast and tax).

€€€ = over €180
€€ = €110–180
€ = under €110

Symbol of Perfection
Hotel Arts Barcelona, the highest building in Spain and Barcelona's only waterfront hotel, towers above the entrance to the Port Olímpic. Its post-Modern interior is filled with modern Catalan art and on its waterfront terraces a vast copper fish designed by Frank Gehry (▶ 74) has become a new symbol of the city.

Hotel Construction
Several hotels have recently been constructed at the top of La Rambla, in an attempt to revitalise this famous street. The apartment-style Citadines, designed by Esteve Bonnell, is one of the more attractive (➤ 101).

www.nnhotels.es
✉ Gran Via de les Cortes Catalanes 642 ☎ 93 318 19 00
🚇 Catalunya

Gravina (€€)
This charming 3-star hotel has a prime location near the bustling Plaça de Catalunya.
www.hotel-gravina.com
✉ Carrer Gravina 12 ☎ 93 301 68 68 🚇 Universitat

Jardí (€)
A small, friendly hotel with clean, simple rooms overlooking two of the Barri Gòtic's prettiest squares, Plaça Sant Josep Oriol and Plaça del Pi.
✉ Plaça Sant Josep Oriol 1 ☎ 93 301 59 00 🚇 Liceu

Méson Castilla (€)
A quiet, characterful family-run hotel on the edge of the old town, with 56 rooms furnished in traditional style.
www.mesoncastilla.com
✉ Carrer Valldonzella 5
☎ 93 318 21 82
🚇 Universitat

Oriente (€€)
The Oriente was once *the* place to stay in Barcelona. Restored but still traditionally furnished, it draws those seeking a taste of history.
www.husa.es
✉ La Rambla 45 ☎ 93 302 25 58 🚇 Liceu

Rey Juan Carlos I Conrad International (€€€)
A member of the 'Leading Hotels of the World' group, set in private gardens and with extensive views of the city. First-rate facilities.
www.hrjuancarlos.com
✉ Avinguda Diagonal 661–671
☎ 93 364 40 40
🚇 Zona Universitària

Rialto (€)
The cosy atmosphere and bedrooms stylishly furnished with Catalan flair makes this 3-star hotel in the Barri Gòtic an excellent choice.
www.gargallo-hotels.com
✉ Carrer Ferran 42 ☎ 93 318 52 12 🚇 Jaume I

Ritz (€€€)
Part of the 'Leading Hotels ofthe World' group, this hotel has gracious old-world charm, solicitous staff and a reputation for excellent cuisine and service.
www.rtizbcn.com
✉ Gran Via de les Corts Catalanes 668 ☎ 93 510 1130
🚇 Passeig de Gràcia

Rivoli Rambla (€€€)
Opened in 1989, this hotel immediately established itself as one of the best. Behind the dignified *Modernista* façade, the interior contains murals, art deco furnishings and many antiques. A rooftop terrace overlooks the smarter end of La Rambla.
www.rivolihotels.com
✉ La Rambla 128 ☎ 93 302 66 43 🚇 Catalunya

Roma Reial (€)
Excellent, cheap accommodation overlooking the Plaça Reial. Service is friendly and all rooms have bathroom and phone.
✉ Plaça Reial 11 ☎ 93 302 03 66 🚇 Liceu

Sant Agustí (€)
Just off La Rambla, and near Boqueria market, this smart, modern 3-star hotel offers excellent value in a quiet yet central location.
www.hotelsa.com
✉ Plaça Sant Agustí 3
☎ 93 318 16 58 🚇 Liceu

Catalonia

Figueres

Ampurdan (€€)
This stylish hotel, just north of Figueres, was the birthplace of the new Catalan cuisine and is still a place of pilgrimage for food-lovers.
☒ **Antiga Carretera de França** ☎ **972 50 05 62**

Hotel Durán (€€)
This popular hotel also has a highly regarded restaurant, that serves hearty traditional cuisine with a modern touch. Was a favourite haunt of Salvador Dalí and friends.
wwwhotelduran.com
☒ **Carrer Lasuaca 5** ☎ **972 50 12 50**

Girona

Bellmirall (€)
Characterful hotel, housed inside the ancient buildings of the Jewish quarter and near to the cathedral. Feels more like a country dwelling.
☒ **Carrer Bellmirall 3** ☎ **972 20 40 09**

Carlemany (€€€)
Smart, modern hotel between the station and the old town, and brimful of modern art. Its restaurant is one of the best in town.
www.carlemany.es
☒ **Plaça Miquel Santaló** ☎ **972 21 12 12**

Montserrat

Abat Cisneros (€€)
The name of this 3-star hotel, set in Montserrat's main square, is derived from a title given to the head of Benedictine monasteries during the Middle Ages. It has cheap, basic rooms in the former monks' cells.
www.abadiamontserrat.net
☒ **Plaça de Monestir, 08199 Montserrat** ☎ **93 877 77 01;**

Sitges

Capri-Veracruz (€–€€)
Excellent value just off the seafront, this family-run hotel consists of two houses which sandwich a small garden with an outdoor pool, Jacuzzi and terrace.
☒ **Avinguda Sofia 13–17** ☎ **93 811 02 67**

Celimar (€–€€)
A recently renovated 3-star *Modernista* hotel, with 26 rooms just a stone's throw from the beach. Ask for one with a balcony.
www.hotelcelimar.com
☒ **Passeig de Ribera 20** ☎ **93 811 01 70**

El Xalet (€)
A discreet hotel in a beautiful *Modernista* villa, with just 10 well-furnished rooms, restaurant, pool and garden.
☒ **Carrer Isla de Cuba 35** ☎ **93 811 0070**

Tarragona

Fòrum (€)
Simple, clean rooms overlooking Plaça de la Font in the Old Town, above a jolly *bodega*-style restaurant.
☒ **Plaça de la Font 37** ☎ **977 23 17 18**

Imperial Tarraco (€€)
Tarragona's top hotel (4-star), centrally situated and overlooking both the sea and the Amfiteatre Romà (► 88).
www.husa.es ☒ **Passeig de Palmeres** ☎ **977 23 30 40;**

Urbis (€)
Reasonably priced, friendly 3-star hotel in the town centre, just off the Rambla Nova and near the daily fruit market.
☒ **Carrer Reding 20 bis** ☎ **977 24 01 16**

Hotel Choices
It is advisable to make reservations in advance throughout Catalonia, especially in the cities and the coastal regions. Two types of accommodation are available – hotels (H) and pensions (P). Hotels are classified from 1- to 5-star, while pensions have 1 or 2 stars. As hotel standards vary considerably, view the room before committing yourself.

Clothes, Jewellery & Accessories

Department Stores and Malls

El Corte Inglés is the city's foremost department store, with several different locations (Plaça Catalunya, Plaça Francesc Macià, Avinguda Diagonal 617–6 and 471–3, and Avinguda Portal de l'Angel 19–21), and particularly strong fashion sections for men, women and children. Fashion malls include La Avenida, a small arcade of luxury shops (✉ Rambla de Catalunya 121), and Bulevard Rosa (✉ Passeig de Gràcia 55). Look out for mega-malls, Barcelona Glóries and L'Illa (✉ Diagonal 208 and 545-557) and Maremagnum, Moll d'Espanya s/n.

Adolfo Domínguez

One of Spain's most famous designers, Adolfo Domínguez is renowned for introducing linen suits in the 1980s with the slogan 'wrinkles are fashionable'. He also designed this shop.

✉ **Passeig de Gràcia 32**
☎ 93 487 41 70 🚇 **Passeig de Gràcia**

Alea

Splendid showcase for up-and-coming Catalan jewellers in the newly trendy district of La Ribera.

✉ **Carrer Argenteria 66**
☎ 93 310 13 73 🚇 **Jaume I, Barceloneta**

Antonio Miró

Antonio Miró is Spain's brightest young fashion star. Although best known for his men's fashions, he also designs women's and children's clothes, shoes, spectacles and furniture.

✉ **Carrer Consell de Cent 349–351** ☎ 93 487 06 70
🚇 **Passeig de Gràcia**

0,925 Argenters

Small, chic jewellery shop near the Picasso Museum featuring work in gold, silver, platinum and steel from four young Spanish designers.

✉ **Carrer Montcada 25** ☎ 93 319 43 18 🚇 **Jaume I**

Bagués

Run by an old family of gold and silversmiths, this shop on the ground floor of Casa Amatller (▶ 36) contains priceless works by Masriera, the sole creator of the *Modernista* style in the Spanish jewellery trade.

✉ **Passeig de Gràcia 41**
☎ 93 216 01 73 🚇 **Passeig de Gràcia**

Bóboli

A leading Spanish brand for children and teens clothing. Comfortable, stylish and sporty.

✉ **Carrer Gran de Gràcia 98**
☎ 93 237 56 70 🚇 **Gràcia**

Carles Galindo

Stylish shop-cum-showroom featuring local designer Carles Galindo's striking collection of accessories for both sexes – handbags, belts and jewellery often made from unusual materials.

✉ **Carrer Verdi 56** ☎ 93 416 07 04 🚇 **Lesseps**

Corbata Barcelona

An astonishing range of ties are on sale in this tiny shop at Port Vell.

✉ **Moll d'Espanya s/n, Maremagnum** ☎ 93 225 81 32
🚇 **Drassanes**

Cristina Castaner

All the latest trends in women's footwear, plus handbags and other accessories.

✉ **Carrer Mestre Nicolau 23**
☎ 93 414 24 28 🚇 **Maria Cristina, Hospital Clínic**

Joaquín Berao

Jewellery by Joaquín Berao, celebrated for his unusual combinations of materials and avant-garde chunky designs.

✉ **Rambla de Catalunya 74**
☎ 93 215 00 91 🚇 **Diagonal**

Lydia Delgado

Delgado is one of Barcelona's most distinctive local designers of easy-to-wear women's fashions. Her collections are sold in this shop alone.

✉ **Carrer Minerva 21** ☎ 93 415 99 98 🚇 **Gràcia, Diagonal**

Loewe

One of the most celebrated leather-goods companies in the world, located in Domènech i Montaner's *Modernista* Lleó-Morera building.

✉ **Passeig de Gràcia 35**
☎ **93 216 04 00** 🚇 **Passeig de Gràcia**

Mango

This chainstore brims with cheap, trendy designs for the truly fashionable. Several branches around Barcelona, include a particularly large one at Passeig de Gràcia 65 and another inside the L'Illa Diagonal shopping mall.

✉ **Avinguda Portal de l'Àngel 7** ☎ **93 317 69 85** 🚇 **Catalunya**

La Manual Alpargatera

This shop has been making traditional Spanish espadrilles, with esparto soles, by hand since 1910. Their footwear has been worn by celebrities as diverse as Michael Douglas, Jack Nicholson and the Pope.

✉ **Carrer Avinyó 7** ☎ **93 301 01 72** 🚇 **Jaume I, Liceu**

Mokuba

A specialist shop which seems dominated by the rows and rows of ribbons and braids. It must be every haberdasher's dream to come to a place like this!

✉ **Carrer Consell de Cent 329** ☎ **93 488 12 77** 🚇 **Universitat**

Muxart Chic

This is a vibrant shop showcasing shoes by Barcelonan shoe designer, Muxart.

✉ **Carrer Rosselló 230**

☎ **93 488 10 64** 🚇 **Provença, Diagonal** ✉ **Rambla Catalunya 47** 🚇 **Catalunya**

Noel Barcelona

All the latest trends in footwear, from thigh boots to not-very-sensible-but-fun platform trainers.

✉ **Carrer Pelai 46** ☎ **93 317 86 38** 🚇 **Catalunya, Universitat**

Pedro Alonso

This small shop with its gloves, fans and imitation jewellery, once catered mainly for stage performers, but today has a more diverse clientele.

✉ **Carrer Santa Anna 27** ☎ **93 317 60 85** 🚇 **Catalunya**

La Perla Gris

Lingerie, swimwear and corsetry from all the best brands.

✉ **Rambla Catalunya 112** ☎ **93 218 07 96** 🚇 **Diagonal**

Regia

This is Barcelona's prime perfumery and it even has its own small 'Perfume Museum' at the back of the shop, which may be visited by appointment.

✉ **Passeig de Gràcia 39** ☎ **93 216 01 21** 🚇 **Passeig de Gràcia**

Sole

Shoes, boots and sandals made of fine Moroccan and Spanish leather, including Spanish cowboy boots.

✉ **Carrer Ample 7** ☎ **93 301 69 84** 🚇 **Drassnes**

Zara

A nationwide chain of trendy fashion stores, popular with young shoppers.

✉ **Carrer Pelai 58** ☎ **93 301 09 78** 🚇 **Catalunya**

Streetwise

Barcelona has two main shopping areas. The Ciutat Vella contains many traditional shops as well as more off-beat boutiques. Try Carrer Banys Nous for arts and antique shops; Carrer Petritxol for home accessories and gift ideas; Carrer Portaferrissa and Carrer Portal de l'Angel for fashion and shoes. The Eixample's three main streets – Passeig de Gràcia, Rambla de Catalunya and the Diagonal – are a showcase for the latest in fashion and design.

Art, Crafts, Gifts & Design

Museum Shops
Barcelona's museum shops stock a high-quality selection of goods such as designer items, gifts and arty souvenirs. Fundació Miró or Museu Picasso both offer a large array of fine products devoted to these artists; La Pedrera shows *Modernista* jewellery and other Gaudí-inspired gifts; and MACBA is one of the main outlets for the quality 'Made in Barcelona' range of gifts and souvenirs.

Ajupa't
Hidden through a low, arched doorway, this small shop is a veritable treasure trove of original gift ideas, including chunky local jewellery, handicrafts, papier mâché and paper goods.
✉ **Carrer València 261** ☎ **93 488 24 13** Ⓜ **Passeig de Gràcia**

Art Escudellers
Huge emporium selling Spanish pottery and ceramics, from factory pieces to arty individual designs. In the basement are a wine cellar, delicatessen and wine bar where you can sample the local products.
✉ **Carrer Escudellers 23** ☎ **93 412 68 01** Ⓞ **Daily 11–11** Ⓜ **Liceu, Drassanes**

Atalanta Manufactura
Just behind Santa Maria del Mar, a husband-and-wife team from Madrid paint beautiful silk scarves, often inspired by local art and architecture. Personalised designs upon request.
✉ **Passeig del Born 10** ☎ **93 268 37 02** Ⓜ **Jaume 1**

Baraka
A treasure trove of Moroccan souvenirs with a wide range of gift ideas from hookah pipes and incense, to jewellery and mirrored, embroidered blouses.
✉ **Carrer Canvis Vells 2** ☎ **93 268 42 20** Ⓜ **Jaume 1**

BD Ediciones de Diseno
Winner of several awards for its state-of-the-art furniture and household design, beautifully displayed in a striking *Modernista* house by Domènech i Montaner.
✉ **Carrer Mallorca 291** ☎ **93 458 69 09** Ⓜ **Diagonal**

Centre Catal d'Artesania
The impressive centre of Catalan handicrafts contains some of the finest ceramics, jewellery, textiles, sculptures and glassware of the region.
✉ **Passeig de Gràcia 55** ☎ **93 467 46 60** Ⓜ **Passeig de Gràcia**

Cereria Subirà
The oldest shop in the city, founded in 1761, selling candles ancient and modern, religious and profane.
✉ **Baixada Llibreteria 7** ☎ **93 315 26 06** Ⓜ **Jaume I**

Coses de Casa
Handmade patchwork quilts and fabrics, including the distinctive Mallorcan *roba de llengües* (literally 'cloth of tongues'), striking for its red, blue or green zigzag patterns.
✉ **Plaça Sant Josep Oriol 5** ☎ **93 302 73 28** Ⓜ **Jaume I**

Germanes Garcia
Wickerwork of all shapes and sizes tumbles out of this village-style shop into the streets of the Old City.
✉ **Carrer Banys Nous 15** ☎ **93 318 66 46** Ⓜ **Liceu**

Ici et La
Interesting, exotic shop stocking new furniture, lighting and accessories by young Spanish designers.
✉ **Plaça Santa Maria del Mar 2** ☎ **93 268 11 67** Ⓜ **Jaume 1**

D Barcelona
A wide choice of gifts and avant-garde household items, together with temporary exhibitions presenting the work of young designers as well as some of the more established names.

✉ **Avinguda Diagonal 367**
☎ 93 216 03 46 🚇 **Diagonal**

Dos I Una
The first design shop in
Barcelona – a tiny treasure
trove of gadgets and unusual
gift ideas.
✉ **Carrer Rosselló 275** ☎ 93
217 70 32 🚇 **Diagonal**

Galeria Maeght
Come to these specialists in
20th-century art, design and
photography for posters,
prints and other graphic
works. Upstairs is a
prestigious art gallery.
✉ **Carrer Montcada 25** ☎ 93
301 42 54 🚇 **Liceu, Jaume I**

El Ingenio
Children adore this old-
fashioned magic shop,
where carnival masks and
costumes are created in a
workshop at the back. Come
here for free magic shows
on Thursday afternoons.
✉ **Carrer Rauric 6** ☎ 93 317
71 38 🚇 **Liceu, Jaume I**

Itaca
Folk pottery and crafted
glassware from all parts of
Spain, Mexico and Morocco.
✉ **Carrer Ferran 24–26** ☎ 93
301 30 44 🚇 **Liceu**

La Manual Alpargatera
All kinds of handmade, straw
woven items, including hats,
bags and their speciality,
espadrilles.
✉ **Carrer Avinyó 7** ☎ 93 301
01 72 🚇 **Liceu, Jaume I**

Museu Picasso
One of Barcelona's many
notable museum shops
reflecting the city's
connections with this major
20th century artist (▶ 106,
panel).

✉ **Carrer Montcada 15** ☎ 93
319 63 10 🚇 **Jaume I**

Pilma
This is an expensive store
specialising in top-name
furniture, textiles, household
items and accessories.
✉ **Avinguda Diagonal 403**
☎ 93 416 13 99 🚇 **Diagonal**

Poble Espanyol
Over 60 art and craft shops
in a reproduction 'Spanish
Village' (▶ 22) selling
traditional wares from all
corners of Spain (▶ panel).
✉ **Avinguda del Marqués de
Comillas s/n** ☎ 93 508 63 00
🚌 **13, 61** 🚇 **Espanya**

Puzzlemanía
Over a thousand different
jigsaw puzzles.
✉ **Carrer Diputació 225** ☎ 93
451 58 03 🚇 **Universitat**

El Rey de la Màgica
Stepping inside this
extraordinary magic shop,
founded in 1881 is like
entering another world.
✉ **Carrer la Princessa 11**
☎ 93 319 73 93 🚇 **Jaume I**

Sala Parés
Barcelona's finest gallery –
specialist in 19th- and 20th-
century paintings, drawings
and sculptures.
✉ **Carrer Pextritxol 5** ☎ 93
318 70 20 🚇 **Catalunya**

Vinçon
This design 'department
store' is Barcelona's answer
to Terance Conran. Trendy
yet practical household
articles at accessible prices.
Won the National Design
Prize in 1995.
✉ **Passeig de Gràcia 96**
☎ 93 215 60 50 🚇 **Passeig
de Gràcia**

Poble Espanyol
This purpose-built 'Spanish
Village' (▶ 22), with its
methodically numbered
shops and studios
demonstrating local craft-
making skills, offers a
comprehensive range of
Spanish and Mallorcan
souvenirs. On sale are fine
glassware, wood-carvings,
Lladro porcelain,
decorative goldware and
jewellery together with
flamenco costumes,
guitars, fans and
castanets.

Antiques, Books & Music

Local Alternative to St Valentine's Day

To celebrate the day of Sant Jordi (St George), Catalonia's patron saint, couples express their love by exchanging gifts: roses for the woman and a book for the man. The Ramblas are lined with temporary bookstalls, and half of Catalonia's annual book sales take place on this day.

Angel Batlle

Antiquarian books, old maps, prints and nautical charts are in abundance here.

✉ **Carrer Palla 23** ☎ **93 301 58 84** Ⓜ **Liceu**

L'Arca de l'Avia

An Aladdin's cave of antique cottons, linens, silks. Beautiful, albeit pricey, patchwork eiderdowns and beaded bags.

✉ **Carrer Banys Nous 20** ☎ **93 302 15 98** Ⓜ **Liceu**

Artur Ramon Anticuario

Two adjacent premises displaying a wide array of antique paintings, sculpture and decorative arts.

✉ **Carrer de la Palla 25** ☎ **93 302 59 70** Ⓜ **Jaume I**

Born Subastas

This auction house holds sales every other week, but it's always an interesting place in which to browse.

✉ **Passeig Sant Joan 60** ☎ **93 268 34 55** Ⓜ **Tetaun**

Bulevard dels Antiquaris

Spacious mall containing over 70 shops for art-lovers and antique collectors. Don't miss Ivan's (☎ 93 215 94 09), with its porcelain doll collection, or Turn of the Century (☎ 93 215 94 63) for decorative *Modernista* pieces.

✉ **Passeig de Gràcia 55** ☎ **93 215 44 99** Ⓜ **Passeig de Gràcia**

Casa Beethoven

Founded in 1915, this shop carries scores and sheet music. Specialising in pieces by Spanish and Catalan composers.

✉ **La Rambla 97** ☎ **93 301 48 26** Ⓜ **Liceu**

Castelló

A chain of record shops. Carrer Tallers 3 has a huge selection of pop, rock, jazz, blues and soul. No 7 is devoted to classical music.

✉ **Carrer Tallers 3 & 7** ☎ **93 302 59 46** Ⓜ **Catalunya**

FNAC

A book megastore inside El Triangle shopping mall. Two floors of books, videos, CDs, computers, PlayStations, video games and magazines from all over the world.

✉ **Plaça de Catalunya** ☎ **93 344 18 00** Ⓒ **Mon–Sat 10–10** Ⓜ **Catalunya**

Jordi Capell – Cooperative d'Arquitectes

Specialist bookshop for architecture and design, in the basement of the College of Architects.

✉ **Plaça Nova 5** ☎ **93 481 35 60** Ⓜ **Jaume I, Liceu**

Laie

The best selection of English-language books in Barcelona, including travel maps and guides. Has a café upstairs.

✉ **Carrer Pau Claris 85** ☎ **93 318 17 39** Ⓒ **Café: Mon– Sat 9–1** Ⓜ **Urquinaona**

Musical Emporium

A small shop (despite its grand name) that specialises in stringed instruments, especially classical guitars.

✉ **La Rambla 129** ☎ **93 317 63 38** Ⓜ **Catalunya**

Norma Comics

Barcelona's largest comic shop sells a huge variety of comics from many different genres.

✉ **Passeig de Sant Joan 9** ☎ **93 244 84 20** Ⓜ **Arc de Triomf**

Food & Drink

Brunells Pastisseria

Appears in the *Guinness Book of Records* for making Spain's biggest Easter egg. Try the *torró* (traditional almond fudge), *roques de Montserrat* (meringues) and *carquinyolis* (soft almond biscuits).

✉ **Carrer Princesa 22** ☎ **93 319 68 25** 🚇 **Jaume I**

Casa Gispert

Dried fruits, spices, cocoa, coffee, and nuts which are toasted daily in a traditional oak-fired oven.

✉ **Carrer Sombrerers 23**
☎ **93 319 75 35** 🚇 **Jaume I**

Colmado Quillez

Barcelona's most famous traditional grocery store, selling an exceptional array of tinned foods, preserves, cold meats and wines.

✉ **Rambla de Catalunya 63**
☎ **93 215 23 56** 🚇 **Passeig de Gràcia**

Escribà Patisseries

Important *Modernista* artists collaborated on the design of this shop. Celebrated for its monumental chocolate cakes.

✉ **La Rambla 83** ☎ **93 301 60 27** 🚇 **Liceu**

Formatería Cirera

A little out of the way but worth a visit, this specialist cheese store sells many unusual Spanish cheeses.

✉ **Carrer Cera 45** ☎ **93 441 07 59** 🚇 **Sant Antoni**

Forn de Pa Sant Jordi

The long queue outside this bakery is testimony to its excellence. Be sure to taste their *tortellet de cabell d'angel*, a crumbly tart filled with 'angel's hair' (spun candied fruit).

✉ **Carrer Llibreteria 8** ☎ **93 310 40 16** 🚇 **Jaume I**

Herboristeria del Rei

A beautiful shop, crammed with lotions, potions, herbs and spices. Pick up anything from a cup of camomile tea to love spells.

Carrer Vidre 1 ☎ **93 318 05 12** 🚇 **Liceu**

Jamón Jamón

As the name suggests, this shop sells hams and other cold cuts (► panel). There is also a restaurant upstairs.

✉ **Carrer Mestre Nicolau 4**
🚌 **41**

Murrià

This *Modernista* store first opened in 1898, and today sells a wide assortment of cheeses, *charcuterie* and other delicacies.

✉ **Carrer Roger de Llúria 85**
☎ **93 215 57 89** 🚇 **Passeig de Gràcia**

Planelles-Donat

Specialists in Spanish nougats, made by artisanal methods. Try the home-made ice creams, too.

✉ **Avinguda Portal de l'Àngel 25 and 27** ☎ **93 317 34 39**
🚇 **Catalunya**

Vins i Caves La Catedral

Wines from all over Spain, with a particularly strong selection from Catalonia.

✉ **Plaça de Ramon Berenguer el Gran 1** ☎ **93 319 07 27**
🚇 **Jaume I**

Xampany

The only shop devoted solely to the sale of *cava* (sparkling wine). More than 100 varieties to choose from.

✉ **Carrer València 200** ☎ **93 453 93 38** 🚇 **Passeig de Gràcia**

Jamón Jamón

Spain is famous for its hams, its cured and smoked meats and its sausages. The quality of ham varies considerably. Expect to pay up to €84 a kilo for the best, traditionally cured *jamón Jabugo*. Look out also for the classic, cheaper haunches of *jamón serrano* and *jamón Iberico*, and be sure to try *salchichón*, piquant *chorizo*, Catalan *botifarra* and spicy Mallorcan *sobresada* sausages.

Children's Attractions

Parks for Children

Most city parks have attractions for children: Parc de l'Espanya Industrial (➤ 65) has a giant dragon slide and a small boating lake; Parc del Laberint (➤ 66–67) has a topiary maze; Turó Parc holds puppet shows at noon on Sundays in summer; Parc del Castell de l'Oreneta offers miniature train and pony rides on Sunday mornings in summer; Parc de la Ciutadella (➤ 64) contains several play areas, a small boating lake and a zoo.

L'Aquàrium

Barcelona's state-of-the-art aquarium is one of the finest in Europe. As well as the aquatic life on display in 21 tanks, the highlight for most children is the impressive 80m-long tunnel which runs straight through the middle of the shark tank (➤ 72). Upstairs, Explora! has games and activities.

✉ Moll d'Espanya, Port Vell ☎ 93 221 74 74 🕐 Jul–Aug 9:30AM–11PM; Jun–Sep and weekends 9:30AM–9:30PM; rest of the year 9:30AM–9PM 🚊 Good 🚇 Barceloneta, Drassanes 💵 Very expensive

Beaches

With so much to see and do, it is easy to forget the city's 4km of clean, sandy beaches with playgrounds, palm-lined promenades and shower facilities. Very good access for people with disabilities.

✉ Platja de Barceloneta, Nova Icària, Bogatell and La Nova Mar Bella 🚇 Ciutadella, Selva de Mar

Bus Turístic

A circuit around the city on the Bus Turístic with 18 stops at key points of interest is an enjoyable way to see the sights. There are two routes, the northern (red) and southern (blue), and you can hop on and off and change routes as often as you like. The ticket also gives discounts to various attractions as well as the Golondrinas pleasure boats (➤ below) and the Tibidabo tram.

✉ Plaça de Catalunya (or any of its 18 stops) 🕐 First bus leaves Plaça de Catalunya at 9AM 🚇 Catalunya ❓ Tickets for 1 day or 2 days.

Golondrinas (Pleasure Boats, ➤ 72)

A pleasure boat tour of the old harbour or the Port Olímpic is fun for all the family and provides a breath of fresh sea air. The most fun is a trip out to the breakwater on one of the old wooden 'swallow boats', which have been operating since 1888.

✉ Moll de les Drassanes Plaça Portal de la Pau ☎ 93 442 31 06 🕐 Harbour trips operate regularly in summer and once an hour on winter weekends. Trips to the Port Olímpic in a modern covered vessel take place throughout the year, several times daily from Easter to October. 🚇 Drassanes 💵 Moderate

Illa de Fantasia

Europe's largest water park is just north of Barcelona on the coast near Mataró. Daily bus from Estació de Sants and Plaça Universitat (☎ 93 451 27 72 for bus details).

✉ Carrer Vilassar de Dalt ☎ 93 751 45 53 🕐 Jun to mid-Sep 10–7 💵 Very expensive

IMAX Cinema

Older children will enjoy the nature films on IMAX's giant 3-D screen (➤ 72).

✉ Moll d'Espanya, Port Vell ☎ 93 225 11 11 🚇 Barceloneta, Drassanes

Museu de la Ciència

The Museu de la Ciència (Science Museum), one of Barcelona's most popular museums, is currently undergoing a major overhaul due to be completed early in 2004. Among the attractions, children can lift a hippopotamus, ride on a human gyroscope, feel an earthquake and watch the world turn. Special one-hour guided sessions are given daily. Phone for details.

✉ Carrer Teodor Roviralta 55 ☎ 93 212 60 50 ⏰ Tue–Sun 10AM–8PM. Closed Mon. Planetarium shows: Tue–Fri 1, 6; weekends every 45 mins starting at 11.15 ♿ Good 🚌 Avinguda Tibidabo 🚍 17, 22, 58, 60, 73, 85 💵 Moderate

Museu de la Cera

The Waxwork Museum is ideal for a rainy day. Pinocchio, Superman and other heroes are all here and don't miss the horror hall!

✉ Passeig de la Banca, 7 ☎ 93 317 26 49 ⏰ Jul–Sep daily 10–10. Oct–Jun Mon–Fri 10–1:30, 4–7:30; weekends & hols 11–2, 4:30–8 🚇 Drassanes, Liceu 💵 Expensive

Museu del Futbol Club Barcelona (➤ 55)

A must for all children who are keen on football at this holiest of shrines to the glorious game.

✉ Nou Camp – Gate 7 or 9 Carrer Arístides Maillol ☎ 93 496 36 00 ⏰ Mon–Sat 10–6:30; Sun and hols 10–2 🍴 Café (€)

Parc Zoològic

Spain's top zoo boasts over 7,000 animals of 500 different species and has a gorilla exhibition commemorating Snowflake who was the world's only captive albino gorilla. There is also a zoo for the under-fives, where children can stroke farm animals and pets, and a dolphinarium which stages spectacular shows (⏰ Mon–Fri 11:30,

1:30, 4, Sat, Sun and hols 12, 1:30, 4).

✉ Parc de la Ciutadella ☎ 93 225 67 80 ⏰ Summer daily 9:30AM–7:30PM; Winter daily 10–5 ♿ Good 🚇 Ciutadella 💵 Very expensive

Poble Espanyol (➤ 22)

Children enjoy this open-air 'museum', especially on *festa* days.

Port Aventura

Catalonia's answer to Disneyland, and reputedly one of Europe's biggest and best theme parks (➤ panel) has been taken over by Universal Studios. Part of the attraction is the introduction of cartoon characters and a ride called *Sea Odyssey*, a graphic simulated underwater journey with computer animation.

✉ Port Aventura, near Salou ☎ 977 77 90 90 ⏰ Mar–Oct Mon–Fri 10–7, Sat and Sun 10–10; mid-June to mid-Sep daily 10–2AM ♿ Good 🚉 Port Aventura 💵 Expensive

Tibidabo Amusement Park

The charm of this recently renovated fairground, nicknamed *La Muntanya Màgica* (The Magic Mountain), is its authentic, old-fashioned funfair atmosphere with carousels, bumper cars, a hall of mirrors and a breathtaking open ferris wheel (➤ 73). Getting there, on the ancient Tramvia Blau tramline and then by funicular, is exciting in itself.

✉ Parc d'Atraccions del Tibidabo, Plaça Tibidabo 3–4 ☎ 93 211 79 42 ⏰ Call for opening times. Closed mid-Sep to Mar 🚠 Funicular del Tibidabo 💵 Moderate

Port Aventura

This spectacular theme park south of Barcelona on the Costa Daurada promises an entertaining day out for all the family with special shops, restaurants, shows and fairground rides in exotic Mexican, Chinese, Polynesian, Wild Western and Mediterranean settings. Top attractions are the 'typhoon' corkscrew ride and the eight 360° loops of the Dragon Khan, Europe's largest roller-coaster.

Bars, Clubs & Live Music

When in Spain ...
Barcelonans are night owls, especially on Thursdays, Fridays and Saturdays. The evening begins around 8:30PM with a *passeig* (promenade), followed by *tapas* in a local bar, then dinner at around 10:30PM. Opera, ballet and concerts usually start at 9PM, and the theatre at 10PM. After midnight, music bars become crowded. Around 3AM, clubs and discos fill up and the famous Barcelonan night movement – *la movida* – sweeps across the city until dawn.

Bikini
One of Barcelona's best night spots, with a popular rock/disco club, a Latin-American salsa room and a classy cocktail lounge.
✉ **Carrer Deu i Mata 105**
☎ **93 322 08 00**
🕐 **Tue–Sat from midnight**
🚇 **Les Corts, Maria Cristina**

La Bolsa
An unusual bar which lets you play the market at 'The Stock Exchange', where the drink prices fluctuate according to a drink's popularity that night.
✉ **Carrer Tuset 17**
☎ **93 202 26 35** 🚇 **Gràcia, Diagonal**

Buena Vista
Barcelona's most authentic salsa club, with free classes on Wed and Thu at 10:30PM and dancing partners at weekends to take you through the cha-cha-cha.
✉ **Carrer Rosselló 217**
☎ **93 237 65 28** 🕐 **Wed–Thu 10:30PM–4AM, Fri and Sat 11PM–5:30 AM, Sun 8PM–1AM**
🚇 **Diagonal**

La Cova del Drac
The city's top jazz venue.
✉ **Carrer Vallmajor 33** ☎ **93 200 70 32** 🕐 **Closed Sun and Mon** 🚇 **Muntaner**

Danzatoria
With its restaurant, disco, beautiful terrace café and rambling gardens on the slopes of Tibidabo, this sophisticated establishment is a favourite summer venue, despite the lengthy uphill trek from the station.
✉ **Avinguda Tibidabo 61**
☎ **93 206 49 501**
🕐 **Tue–Sun 7PM–3AM**
🚇 **Tibidabo**

Estadi Olímpic
Main venue for mega-star pop concerts. Tickets best bought through record shops.
✉ **Passeig Olímpic** ☎ **93 425 49 49** 🚌 **61**

Harlem Jazz Club
Small, but very atmospheric jazz club – has long been a favourite of jazz aficionados.
✉ **Carrer Comtessa de Sobradiel 8** ☎ **93 310 07 55**
🕐 **Tue–Sun 8PM–4AM**
🚇 **Jaume I**

Jamboree
A choice nightspot for blues, soul, jazz, funk and occasional hip-hop live bands. Upstairs is Los Tarantos, a laid-back bar with predominantly Spanish music.
✉ **Plaça Reial** ☎ **93 301 75 64** 🕐 **Daily from 11PM**
🚇 **Liceu**

Marsella
In stark contrast to Barcelona's many design bars, this traditional bar in the Barri Xines has been run by the same family for five generations and still serves locally made absinthe (*absenta*).
✉ **Carrer Sant Pau 65** ☎ **93 442 72 63** 🕐 **Mon–Thu 9PM–2:30AM, Fri–Sun 5PM–3:30AM**
🚇 **Liceu**

Nayandei Boîte
The biggest of the discos on the roof terrace of the Maremagnum complex. The Nayadei Boîte is always teeming with teenagers.
✉ **Maremagnum, Port Vell**
☎ **93 225 80 10** 🕐 **Mon–Sat 9PM–5AM, Sun 6PM–5AM**
🚇 **Barceloneta, Drassanes**

Nick Havanna
One of Barcelona's most

talked-about bars, thanks to its sensational design. Go late.

✉ **Carrer Rosselló 208** ☎ **93 217 77 32** 🕐 **Daily 11PM–4AM (5AM Fri and Sat)** 🚇 **Diagonal**

Nitsa

One of the city's best-loved clubs for indie-rock, breakbeat and techno, in a funky dance hall.

✉ **Nou de la Rambla 113** ☎ **93 301 00 90** 🕐 **Fri & Sat, 12:30–6AM** 🚌 **17, 39, 45, 57, 59, 64**

Otto Zutz

This is one of the smartest clubs in town, and a *tour de force* of design, with its clever lighting and metal staircases and galleries. Dress smartly and arrive after midnight.

✉ **Carrer Lincoln 15** ☎ **93 238 07 22** 🕐 **Wed–Sun midnight–6AM** 🚇 **Fontana, Passeig de Gràcia**

La Paloma

Foxtrots, tangos and boleros are still *de rigueur* at the city's famous dance hall.

✉ **Carrer Tigre 27** ☎ **93 317 79 94** 🕐 **Thu– Sun 6–9:30PM, 11:30PM–5AM** 🚇 **Universitat**

Pastis

Small, dimly lit bohemian bar. Sip *pastis* accompanied by Edith Piaf songs played on a phonograph.

✉ **Calle Santa Mònica 4** ☎ **93 318 79 80** 🕐 **Mon, Wed–Sun 7:30PM–2:30AM (Fri till 3:30AM); closed Tue** 🚇 **Drassanes**

La Terrazza

Summertime open-air club on Montjuïc mountain, behind Poble Espanyol. Gets crowded around 3 or 4AM.

✉ **Avinguda Marquès de Comillas, Montjuïc** ☎ **93 423 12 85** 🕐 **Fri–Sat midnight–6AM** 🚌 **61**

Torres de Ávila

Design-bar in the Poble Espanyol. Trance-techno discos are staged here at weekends and, in summer, the rooftop terrace bars are particularly magical.

✉ **Avinguda Marquès de Comillas, Poble Espanyol, Montjuïc** ☎ **93 424 93 09** 🕐 **Fri, Sat and Sun from 11PM** 🚇 **Espanya**

Tres Torres

Beautiful gardens and an elegant courtyard create a sophisticated background for a moneyed clientele. On Thursday nights there is often live jazz or blues.

✉ **Via Augusta 300** ☎ **93 205 16 08** 🕐 **Mon–Sat 7PM–3AM** 🚇 **Tres Torres**

Up And Down

Barcelona's most exclusive nightclub. 'Up'stairs, an affluent, black-tie, post-opera crowd dance, while 'down'stairs, their well-dressed offspring enjoy contemporary club music.

✉ **Carrer Numància 179** ☎ **93 205 51 94** 🕐 **Disco: Tue–Sat 12AM–5:30 or 6AM** 🚇 **Sants Estació** ❓ **Men must wear a tie**

Xampanyería Casablanca

Catalan champagne bar near the Passeig de Gràcia serving four kinds of house *cava* by the glass as well as a wide range of tasty *tapas* snacks (▶ panel).

✉ **Carrer Bonavista 6** ☎ **93 237 63 99** 🕐 **Thu–Sat 8PM–2:30AM; (3AM Fri & Sat)** 🚇 **Passeig de Gràcia**

Barcelona's 'Bubbly'

Over 50 Spanish companies produce champagne. Look out for Gramona, Mestres and Torello labels. Catalan champagne is called *cava*, and champagne bars are known as *xampanyerías*. Most serve a limited selection of house *cavas* by the glass, *brut* or *brut nature* (*brut* is slightly sweeter), accompanied by *tapas*. Xampanyet (✉ Carrer Montcada 22), Xampanyería Casablanca and La Bodegueta del Xampú (✉ Gran Via de les Corts Catalanes 702) are among the most popular.

Theatre, Cinema, Music & Dance

Listings

For entertainment listings, the best source of local information is the magazine *Guía del Ocio*, which previews *La Semana de Barcelona* (This Week in Barcelona). Available from any newsstand, it gives full details (in Spanish) of film, theatre and musical events, and lists bars, restaurants and nightlife. *Informatíu Musical* and the monthly magazine *Barcelona en Música*, available free from tourist offices and record shops, are useful sources of concert information.

Auditori

Barcelona's auditorium was designed by the Spanish architect Rafael Moneo and opened in 1999 as the home of the city's symphony orchestra.

⊠ **Carrer Lepant 150** ☎ **93 247 93 00** Ⓜ **Marina**

Caixa Forum

Host to a plethora of cultural events spanning classical concerts to festivals of poetry.

⊠ **Aviguda del Marquès de Comillas 6–8** ☎ **93 476 8600** Ⓜ **Espanya**

Centre Artesà Tradicionàrius (CAT)

The Centre for Traditional Arts is devoted to the study, teaching and performance of traditional Catalan music and dance.

⊠ **Travessera de Sant Antoni 6–8** ☎ **93 218 44 85** Ⓜ **Fontana**

Filmoteca de la Generalitat De Catalunya

Barcelona's official film theatre shows three films a day. These are usually in VO (original version) ie, not in Spanish. There is also a children's programme at 5PM on Sundays.

⊠ **Cinema Aquitania, Avinguda de Sarrià 31–33** ☎ **93 410 75 90** Ⓒ **Performance: 5, 7:30 and 10PM. Closed hols and Aug** Ⓜ **Hospital Clinic**

Fundació Joan Miró

The Foundation Joan Miró is Spain's main centre for the development of contemporary music and stages a series of concerts (*Nit de Música* – Music Nights) during the summer.

⊠ **Plaça Neptú, Parc de Montjuïc** ☎ **93 329 19 08** Ⓒ **Jun–Sep** 🚌 **61**

Gran Teatre del Liceu

Gutted by fire in 1994 this opera house reopened in 1999. World-famous singers, including the Catalan diva Montserrat Caballé, have performed here.

⊠ **La Rambla 51–59** ☎ **93 485 99 13** Ⓜ **Liceu**

IMAX Cinema (➤ 110)

Mercat de les Flors

Innovative dance, drama and music productions.

⊠ **Carrer Lleida 59** ☎ **93 426 18 75** Ⓜ **Espanya**

Palau de la Música Catalána

Barcelona's main venue for classical music (➤ 59).

⊠ **Carrer Sant Francesc de Paula 2** ☎ **93 295 72 00** Ⓒ **Box office: Mon–Fri 10–9; Sat 3–9**

El Tablao de Carmen

Highly rated flamenco cabaret at the Poble Espanyol. Booking in advance is recommended.

⊠ **Carrer Arcs 9, Poble Espanyol, Montjuïc** ☎ **93 425 46 16** Ⓒ **Tue–Sun 8PM–1AM (2–3AM at weekends)** ❓ **Shows Tue–Sun 9:30. Also 11:30PM on Sat and Sun**

Teatre Nacional de Catalunya

Designed by local architect Ricard Bofill as the centrepiece of a new arts district, this theatre is a showcase for contemporary Catalan dance.

⊠ **Plaça de les Arts 1** ☎ **93 306 57 00** Ⓜ **Glòries**

Sport

Spectator Sports

American Football
Estadi Olímpic
The 'Barcelona Dragons' play against other teams in the World League on Sundays, April–June. Buy tickets on the day at the stadium.
✉ Passeig Olímpic 17–19
☎ 93 425 49 49 🚌 61

Basketball
Joventut
League games on Sunday evenings, and European and Spanish Cup matches midweek, September–May. Book tickets in advance.
✉ Avinguda Alfons XIII-Carrer Ponent 143–161, Badalona
☎ 93 460 20 40 Ⓜ Gorg

Bullfighting
Plaça De Toros Monumental
The Bullring and its museum (► 56) are open only during the bullfighting season (Apr–Sep). Reserve tickets in advance (☎ 93 453 38 21).
✉ Grand Via de les Corts Catalanes 749 ☎ 93 245 58 04
Ⓜ Monumental

Football
Nou Camp – FC Barcelona
No visit to Barcelona is complete without a visit to Nou Camp, Europe's largest stadium (seating 120,000), and its museum (► 55).
✉ Avinguda Aristides Maillol. Museum: Gate 7 or 9 ☎ 93 496 36 00 Ⓜ Collblanc, Maria Cristina

Ice Hockey
FC Barcelona Pista de Gel
Barcelona's only professional ice-hockey team. On non-match days, the rink is open to the public.
✉ Avinguda de Joan XXIII
☎ 93 496 36 00 Ⓜ Maria Cristina, Collblanc

Participatory Sports

Cycling
Un Cotxe Menys
Escorted daytime and evening cycle tours around the city (► 75).
✉ Carrer Esparteria 3 ☎ 93 268 21 05 Ⓜ Jaume 1

Golf
El Prat Golf Club
Just 15km from Barcelona. You will need to present a membership card of a nationally federated club. Phone or write in advance.
✉ Calle Plans de Bon Vila 17, Terrassa, 08820 El Prat de Llobregat ☎ 93 728 10 00

Horse riding
Hipica Severino de Sant Cugat
Riding lessons and treks through the countryside around Sant Cugat and the Sierra de Collserola.
✉ Paseo Colado 12, Sant Cugat del Vallès ☎ 93 674 11 40

Sailing
Base Nàutica de la Mar Bella
Friendly sailing school that also rents catamarans and windsurfers by the hour.
✉ Avinguda Litoral in the port Mar Bella ☎ 93 221 04 32 Ⓜ Ciutadella-Villa Olímpica

Tennis
Vall Parc Club
Fourteen open-air tennis courts on Tibidabo. Racquets (not balls) for hire.
✉ Carretera Sant Cugat s/n
☎ 93 212 67 89 🚌 A6

Tickets
Purchase tickets from the relevant box office or from several ticket offices and booths (taquillas) throughout the city. The Centre d'Informació (✉ Palau de la Virreina, Rambla Sant Josep 99 ☎ 902 10 12 12 🕐 Mon–Thu 8–2:30, Fri 8–2:30, 4:30–7:30) sells tickets for all Ajuntament-sponsored performances. Credit card bookings can be made by phone at other times. The booth on the corner of Carrer Aribau and Gran Via (🕐 Mon-Sat 10:30–1:30, 4–7:30) sells tickets for major pop concerts and most theatre productions.

What's On When

Giants & Big Heads
Dancing giants, dragons, *capgrossos* (big heads) and demons play an important part in traditional Catalan folklore. They feature in many *festes*, especially *La Mercè*, with its eccentric *Ball de Gegants*, a dance of costumed 5m-high giants and grinning papier-mâché 'big heads' which is performed from Drassanes to Ciutadella, and the *Corre Foc* (Fire-Running), when devils and dragons scatter firecrackers in the Ciutat Vella.

January
Reis Mags (5–6 Jan): the Three Kings arrive by boat, then tour the city, showering the crowds with sweets.

February
Santa Eulàlia (12–19 Feb): a series of musical events in honour of one of the city's patron saints.
Carnestoltes: one week of pre-Lenten carnival celebrations and costumed processions come to an end on Ash Wednesday with the symbolic burial of a sardine.

March
Sant Medir de Gràcia (3 Mar): procession of traditionally dressed horsemen from Gràcia who ride over Collserola to the Hermitage of Sant Medir (Saint of Broad Beans) for a bean-feast.

March/April
Setmana Santa: religious services and celebrations for Easter Week include a solemn procession from the church of Sant Augustí on Good Friday. Easter celebrations are particularly important in the areas of the city settled by Spaniards from Andalucia and southern Spain.

April
Sant Jordi (23 Apr): the Catalan alternative to St Valentine's Day (➤ 108, panel).

May
Festa de la Bicicleta (one Sun in May): join the Mayor and 15,000 others on a cycle-ride around the city, in an effort to encourage fewer cars.

June
Midsummer (23–24 June) is a good excuse for huge-scale partying and spectacular fireworks.
Trobada Castellera (mid-June): displays of human-tower building.
International Film Festival (last two weeks)
Flamenco Festival (last two weeks).
Festival del Grec; arts festival (end Jun–Aug).

July
Aplec de la Sardana, Olot; the biggest *Sardana* dancing festival in Catalonia.

August
Festa Major de Gràcia (3rd week of Aug): a popular festival of music, dancing and street celebrations in the Gràcia district (➤ 44–45).

September
Diada de Catalunya (11 Sep): Catalonia's National Day does not mark a victory, but the taking of the city by Felipe V in 1714.
La Mercè (20–24 Sep): boisterous parades and spectacles featuring giants, devils, dragons, big heads and musically choreographed fireworks (➤ panel).
Festa Major de la Barceloneta (1–15 Oct): one of the liveliest district *festes*, with processions and dancing on the beach every night.

October
International Jazz Festival.

December
Christmas festivities include a craft fair outside the cathedral (6–23 Dec) and a crib in Plaça Sant Jaume.

Practical Matters

Above: *a busy bus stop in Plaça de Catalunya*
Below: *the* Bus Turístic *connects the major attractions*

TIME DIFFERENCES

GMT	Barcelona	Germany	USA (NY)	Netherlands	Rest of Spain
12 noon	1PM →	1PM →	7AM ←	1PM →	1PM →

BEFORE YOU GO

WHAT YOU NEED

● Required ○ Suggested ▲ Not required	Some countries require a passport to remain valid for a minimum period (usually at least six months) beyond the date of entry – contact their consulate or embassy or your travel agent for details.	UK	Germany	USA	Netherlands	Spain
Passport or National Identity Card where applicable		●	●	●	●	●
Visa (regulations can change – check before booking your journey)		▲	▲	▲	▲	▲
Onward or Return Ticket		▲	▲	▲	▲	▲
Health Inoculations		▲	▲	▲	▲	▲
Health Documentation (➤ 123)		●	●	●	●	●
Travel Insurance		○	○	○	○	○
Driving Licence (national with Spanish translation or International)		●	●	●	●	●
Car Insurance Certificate (if own car)		●	●	●	●	●
Car registration document (if own car)		●	●	●	●	●

WHEN TO GO

Barcelona

 High season

Low season

14°C	15°C	17°C	19°C	22°C	25°C	29°C	29°C	27°C	23°C	18°C	15°C
JAN	FEB	MAR	APR	MAY	JUN	JUL	AUG	SEP	OCT	NOV	DEC

🌧 Wet   ☁ Cloud   ☀ Sun   🌦 Sunshine & showers

TOURIST OFFICES

In the UK
Spanish Tourist Office
79 New Cavendish Street
London W1W 6XB
☎ (020) 7486 8077
Fax: (020) 7486 8034
www.spain.info

In the USA
Tourist Office of Spain
666 Fifth Avenue (35th floor)
New York
NY 10103
☎ (1212) 265-8822
Fax: (1212) 265-8864

Tourist Office of Spain
8383 Wilshire Boulevard
Suite 960
Beverley Hills
CA 90211
☎ (1213) 658-7192
Fax: (1213) 658-1061

CITY POLICE (POLICÍA MUNICIPAL) 092

NATIONAL POLICE (POLICÍA NACIONAL) 091

FIRE (BOMBEROS) 080

AMBULANCE (AMBULÀNCIA) 061

WHEN YOU ARE THERE

ARRIVING

Spain's national airline, Iberia, has scheduled flights to Barcelona's El Prat de Llobregat Airport from major Spanish and European cities. The city is served by over 30 international airlines including BA, Delta, KLM, Lufthansa and Virgin Express, and has direct flights to more than 80 international destinations.

El Prat de Llobregat Airport Kilometres to city centre	**Journey times**	
	🚋	20 minutes
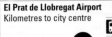	🚌	40 minutes
12 kilometres	🚕	30 minutes

Estacio de França **Railway Station** Near Barceloneta	**Journey times**	
	🚋	available
	🚌	available
Near centre	🚕	available

MONEY

The euro is the official currency of Spain.
Euro banknotes and coins were introduced in January 2002. Spain's former currency, the peseta, went out of circulation in early 2002.
Banknotes are in denominations of 5, 10, 20, 50, 100, 200 and 500 euros; coins are in denominations of 1, 2, 5, 10, 20 and 50 cents, and 1 and 2 euros.
Euro traveller's cheques are widely accepted, as are major credit cards. Credit and debit cards can also be used for withdrawing euro notes from ATMs.

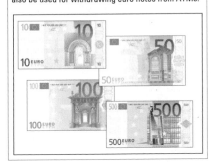

TIME

 Like the rest of Spain, Catalonia is one hour ahead of Greenwich Mean Time (GMT+1), except from late March to late October, when summer time (GMT+2) operates.

CUSTOMS

 YES
From another EU country for personal use (guidelines)
800 cigarettes, 200 cigars, 1 kilogram of tobacco
10 litres of spirits (over 22%)
20 litres of aperitifs
90 litres of wine, of which 60 litres can be sparkling wine
110 litres of beer

From a non-EU country for your personal use, the allowances are:
200 cigarettes OR
50 cigars OR 250 grams of tobacco
1 litre of spirits (over 22%)
2 litres of intermediary products (eg sherry) and sparkling wine
2 litres of still wine
50 grams of perfume
0.25 litres of eau de toilette
The value limit for goods is 175 euros

Travellers under 17 years of age are not entitled to the tobacco and alcohol allowances.

 NO
Drugs, firearms, ammunition, offensive weapons, obscene material, unlicensed animals.

TOURIST OFFICES

Turisme de Barcelona
www.barcelonaturisme.com
- Plaça de Catalunya 17
  ☎ 93 368 97 30
  🕐 Daily 9–9

The main tourist office is situated beneath Plaça de Catalunya. Services include hotel reservations, currency exchange, walking tours and theatre and concert tickets.

There are branches of the city tourist office on the ground floor of the city hall and at the Sants railway station.

- Plaça Sant Jaume I
  🕐 Mon–Sat 10–8, Sun 10–2
- Sants Railway Station (Estació de Sants)
  🕐 Mon–Fri 8–8, Sat–Sun 8–2

There are also tourist information offices in the airport arrival halls, open daily 9–9.

Turisme de Catalunya
- Palau Robert
  Passeig de Gràcia 105
  ☎ 93 238 40 00
  🕐 Mon–Sat 10–7, Sun 10–2

In summer, information booths can be found at Sagrada Família and La Rambla. In the Barrí Gòtic, you may also come across uniformed tourist officials, known as 'Red Jackets'.

NATIONAL HOLIDAYS

J	F	M	A	M	J	J	A	S	O	N	D
2		1(2)	(2)	(1)1	(1)1		1	2	1	1	4

1 Jan	New Year's Day
6 Jan	Three Kings
19 Mar	Sant Josep
Mar/Apr	Good Friday, Easter Monday
1 May	Labour Day
May/Jun	Whit Monday
24 Jun	St John
15 Aug	Assumption
11 Sep	Catalan National Day
24 Sep	Our Lady of Mercy
12 Oct	Hispanitat
1 Nov	All Saints' Day
6 Dec	Constitution Day
8 Dec	Feast of the Immaculate Conception
25 Dec	Christmas
26 Dec	Sant Esteve

OPENING HOURS

○ Shops   ● Churches
● Offices   ◐ Museums
● Banks   ◐ Pharmacies

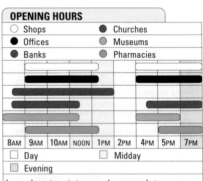

| 8AM | 9AM | 10AM | NOON | 1PM | 2PM | 4PM | 5PM | 7PM |

☐ Day   ☐ Midday
☐ Evening

Large department stores and supermarkets may open outside these times, especially in summer. Business hours also vary depending on the season, with many companies working *horas intensivas* in summer, from 8–3. Banks generally close on Saturdays, although some main branches open in the morning 8:30–12:30. Outside banking hours, money-exchange facilities are available at the airport and Sants railway station. Some *barris* (districts) also have their own separate feast days, when some shops and offices may close.

PUBLIC TRANSPORT

 Metro The metro is the easiest and fastest way of moving around the city. There are two different underground train systems, the Metro with its five lines identified by number and colour, and the FGC (☎ 93 205 15 15) with two lines in Barcelona and four more lines going to nearby towns.

 Buses Barcelona has an excellent bus network; pick up a free plan from any tourist office. Timetables are also shown at individual bus stops. Buses run 5:30AM–11PM. At night there is a *Nitbus* with routes centred on Plaça de Catalunya. Throughout the year the *Bus Turístic*, a hop-on-hop-off service, circuits the main city sights.

Trains The Spanish railway system, RENFE, runs trains from Barcelona to all the major cities in Spain and some outside. Many main-line trains stop at the underground stations at Passeig de Gràcia and Plaça de Catalunya. There are two main railway stations: Estació de Sants and Estació de França near Barceloneta.

Boat Trips The best way to admire the port and coastline is from the sea. Golondrinas offer frequent 35-minute harbour tours or 2-hour voyages to the Port Olímpic (► 33). Although Barcelona is the biggest port in the Mediterranean, the only regular passenger services are to the Balearic islands.

 Cable cars, Funiculars and the Tramvia Blau A cable car connects the lower city with Montjuïc castle and links with the funicular railway. To reach Tibidabo, take the Tramvia Blau (Blue Tram), then the Funicular del Tibidabo to the Amusement Park at the top of the hill.

CAR RENTAL

The leading international car rental companies have offices at Barcelona airport and you can book a car in advance (essential in peak periods) either direct or through a travel agent. Local companies offer competitive rates and will usually deliver a car to the airport.

TAXIS

 Pick up a black and yellow taxi at a taxi rank or hail one if it's displaying a green light and the sign *Lliure/Libre* (free). Fares are not unduly expensive but extra fees are charged for airport trips and for baggage. Prices are shown on a sticker inside.

DRIVING

 Speed limit on motorways (*autopistas*): **120kph**

 Speed limit on main roads : **100kph** On minor roads: **90kph**

 Speed limit in towns (*Poblaciones*): **50kph**

 Seat belts must be worn in front seats at all times and in rear seats where fitted.

 Random breath-testing. Never drive under the influence of alcohol.

 Fuel (*gasolina*) is available as: *Super Plus* (98 octane), *Super* (96 octane), unleaded or *sin plomo* (90 octane) and *gasoleo* or *gasoil* (diesel). Petrol stations are normally open 6AM–10PM, and closed Sundays, though larger ones are open 24 hours. Most take credit cards.

 If you break down driving your own car and are a member of an AIT-affiliated motoring club, you can call the Real Automóvil Club de Catalunya (☎ 93 228 50 00). If the car is hired, follow the instructions given in the documentation; most of the international rental firms provide a rescue service.

PERSONAL SAFETY

The Policía Municipal (navy-blue uniforms) keep law and order in the city. For a police station ask for *la comisaría*.

To help prevent crime:

- Do not carry more cash than you need
- Beware of pickpockets in markets, tourist sights or crowded places
- Avoid walking alone in dark alleys at night, especially in the Barri Xines.
- Leave valuables and important documents in the hotel or apartment safe.

City Police assistance:
☎ **092** from any call box

ELECTRICITY

The power supply is usually 220 volts but a few old buildings are still wired for

125 volts. Sockets accept two-round-pin-style plugs, so an adaptor is needed for most non-Continental appliances and a transformer for appliances operating on 110–120 volts.

TELEPHONES

Public telephones (*teléfono*) still take 25, 100 and 500 peseta coins. They are to be converted to take euros . A phonecard (*credifone*) is available from post offices and tobacconists (*estancs*) for €6.01 or €12.02.

International Dialling Codes	
From Spain to:	
UK:	00 44
Germany:	00 49
USA & Canada:	00 1
Netherlands:	00 31
France:	00 33

Reduced prices apply to calls made between 10PM and 8AM and on Saturdays after 2PM

POST

Most post offices (*correos*) open Mon–Fri, 8:30–2 but some also open in the afternoon and on Saturday morning. The main post office (*Oficina Central*) at Via Laietana 1 is open Mon–Sat 8:30AM–9PM, Sun 8AM–2PM, and the Eixample post office at Carrer Aragó 282 is open Mon–Fri 8AM–9PM and Sat 9–2. You can also buy stamps at any tobacconist (*estanc*).

TIPS/GRATUITIES

Yes ✓ No ✗		
Restaurants (if service not inc.)	✓	10%
Cafés/Bars (if service not inc.)	✓	change
Tour Guides	✓	€1
Hairdressers	✓	change
Taxis	✓	10%
Chambermaids/Porters	✓	€1
Theatre/cinemas usherettes	✓	change
Cloakroom attendants	✓	change
Toilets	✗	

HEALTH

Insurance
Nationals of EU and certain other countries can get medical treatment in Spain with the relevant documentation (Form E111 for Britons), although private medical insurance is still advised and is essential for all other visitors.

Dental Services
Dental treatment is not usually available free of charge as all dentists practise privately. A list of *dentistas* can be found in the yellow pages of the telephone directory. Dental treatment should be covered by private medical insurance.

Sun Advice
The sunniest (and hottest) months are July and August, with an average of 11 hours sun a day and daytime temperatures of 29°C. Particularly during these months you should avoid the midday sun and use a strong sunblock.

Drugs
Prescription and non-prescription drugs and medicines are available from pharmacies (*farmàcias*), distinguished by a large green cross. They are able to dispense many drugs that would be available only on prescription in other countries.

Safe Water
Tap water is generally safe though it can be heavily chlorinated. Mineral water is cheap to buy and is sold as *con gaz* (carbonated) and *sin gaz* (still). Drink plenty of water during hot weather.

CONCESSIONS

Students Holders of an International Student Identity Card (ISIC) may be able to obtain some concessions on travel, entrance fees etc. Most museums offer 50 per cent discount to students, and many are free on the first Sunday of each month. There are several IYHF youth hostels in the city, with accommodation in multi-bed dormitories. Expect to pay around €6–10 per person.

Senior Citizens Barcelona is a popular destination for older travellers, especially during winter. Most museums and galleries offer a 50 per cent discount for retired people.

CLOTHING SIZES

Spain	UK	Europe		
46	36	46	36	
48	38	48	38	
50	40	50	40	
52	42	52	42	Suits
54	44	54	44	
56	46	56	46	
41	7	41	8	
42	7½	42	8½	
43	8½	43	9½	
44	9½	44	10½	Shoes
45	10½	45	11½	
46	11	46	12	
37	14½	37	14½	
38	15	38	15	
39/40	15½	39/40	15½	
41	16	41	16	Shirts
42	16½	42	16½	
43	17	43	17	
36	8	34	6	
38	10	36	8	
40	12	38	10	
42	14	40	12	Dresses
44	16	42	14	
46	18	44	16	
38	4½	38	6	
38	5	38	6½	
39	5½	39	7	
39	6	39	7½	Shoes
40	6½	40	8	
41	7	41	8½	

LANGUAGE

In Barcelona, there are two official languages, Catalan and Spanish, both coming from
Latin but both sounding quite different. Everybody can speak Spanish, although Catalan
is most commonly spoken. At most tourist attractions you will always find someone who
speaks English, and many restaurants have polyglot menus. However, it is advisable to
try to learn at least some Catalan, since English is not as widely spoken as in other
European countries. Here is a basic vocabulary to help you with the most essential
words and expressions.

hotel	*hotel*	chambermaid	*cambrera*
bed and breakfast	*llit i berenar*	bath	*bany*
single room	*habitació senzilla*	shower	*dutxa*
double room	*habitació doble*	washbasin	*lavabo*
one person	*una persona*	toilet	*toaleta*
one night	*una nit*	balcony	*balcó*
reservation	*reservas*	key	*clau*
room service	*servei d'habitació*	lift	*ascensor*

bank	*banc*	exchange rate	*tant per cent*
exchange office	*oficina de canvi*	commission	*comissió*
post office	*correos*	cashier	*caixer*
coin	*moneda*	change	*camvi*
banknote	*bitllet de banc*	foreign	*moneda*
traveller's	*xec de*	currency	*estrangera*
cheque	*viatage*	open	*obert*
credit card	*carta de crèdit*	closed	*tancat*

café	*cafè*	starter	*primer plat*
pub/bar	*celler*	main course	*segón plat*
breakfast	*berenar*	dessert	*postres*
lunch	*dinar*	bill	*cuenta*
dinner	*sopar*	beer	*cervesa*
table	*mesa*	wine	*vi*
waiter	*cambrer*	water	*aigua*
waitress	*cambrera*	coffee	*café*

aeroplane	*avió*	single ticket	*senzill-a*
airport	*aeroport*	return ticket	*anar i tornar*
train	*tren*	non-smoking	*no fumar*
bus	*autobús*	car	*cotxe*
station	*estació*	petrol	*gasolina*
boat	*vaixell*	bus stop	*la parada*
port	*port*	how do I get	*per anar*
ticket	*bitllet*	to...?	*a...?*

yes	*si*	tomorrow	*demà*
no	*no*	excuse me	*perdoni*
please	*per favor*	you're welcome	*de res*
thank you	*gràcies*	how are you?	*com va?*
hello	*hola*	do you speak	*parla*
goodbye	*adéu*	English?	*anglès?*
good morning	*bon dia*	I don't understand	*no ho enten*
good afternoon	*bona tarda*	how much?	*quant es?*
goodnight	*bona nit*	where is...?	*on és...?*
today	*avui*		

INDEX

Acknowledgements

Teresa Fisher wishes to thank Rosemary Trigg of Hotel Arts for her assistance during the research of this book.

The Automobile Association would like to thank the following photographers, libraries, associations and individuals for their assistance in the preparation of this book:
DACS 17; MARY EVANS PICTURE LIBRARY 10b; TERESA FISHER 21b, 38b, 43b, 57a, 58, 70b, 75a, 84b,122a,b,c; HULTON GETTY 14c; MUSEU PICASSO 20b, 20c; NATURE PHOTOGRAPHERS (R Bush) 13a; REX FEATURES 14b; SPECTRUM COLOUR LIBRARY 9c, 25, 27b, 52b, 53c, 87b; WORLD PICTURES 51b; www.euro.ecb.int/ 119 (euro notes).

The remaining pictures are from the Association's own library (AA PHOTO LIBRARY) and were taken by S DAY with the exception of the following:
P ENTICKNAP 5b, 13b, 19b, 23c, 61, 78, 79, 80a, 81, 82, 83, 84a, 85a, 85b, 88a, 88b, 89a, 89b, 90a, 90b, 91a, 92–116; P WILSON 11b, 12b, 17b, 22b, 26b, 26c, 32, 36, 41, 49, 50b, 53b, 55, 59b, 67b, 69b, 73b, 85b, 86.

2005 edition updated by: Word On Spain
Revision management: Pam Stagg

Dear Essential Traveller

**Your comments, opinions and recommendations are very
important to us. So please help us to improve our travel
guides by taking a few minutes to complete this simple
questionnaire.**

*You do not need a stamp (unless posted outside the UK). If you do not want to cut this page
from your guide, then photocopy it or write your answers on a plain sheet of paper.*

Send to: **The Editor, AA World Travel Guides,
FREEPOST SCE 4598, Basingstoke RG21 4GY.**

Your recommendations...

We always encourage readers' recommendations for restaurants, nightlife
or shopping – if your recommendation is used in the next edition of the
guide, we will send you a *FREE* AA *Essential* Guide of your choice.
Please state below the establishment name, location and your reasons
for recommending it.

_____
_____
_____
_____

Please send me **AA *Essential*** _____

About this guide...

Which title did you buy?
 AA *Essential* _____
Where did you buy it? _____
When? m m / y y

Why did you choose an AA *Essential* Guide? _____
_____
_____
_____
_____

Did this guide meet your expectations?
 Exceeded ☐ Met all ☐ Met most ☐ Fell below ☐
 Please give your reasons_____
_____
_____
_____

continued on next page...

Were there any aspects of this guide that you particularly liked? _____
_____
_____

Is there anything we could have done better? _____
_____
_____

About you...

Name (*Mr/Mrs/Ms*) _____
Address _____
_____
_____ Postcode _____
Daytime tel nos _____

Please only give us your mobile phone number if you wish to hear from us
about other products and services from the AA and partners by text or mms.

Which age group are you in?
Under 25 ☐   25–34 ☐   35–44 ☐   45–54 ☐   55–64 ☐   65+ ☐

How many trips do you make a year?
Less than one ☐   One ☐   Two ☐   Three or more ☐

Are you an AA member? Yes ☐   No ☐

About your trip...

When did you book? m m / y y   When did you travel? m m / y y
How long did you stay? _____
Was it for business or leisure? _____
Did you buy any other travel guides for your trip?
    If yes, which ones? _____

Thank you for taking the time to complete this questionnaire. Please send it to us as soon as
possible, and remember, you do not need a stamp (*unless posted outside the UK*).

Happy Holidays!